THE AMERUCAN DREAM

From a Leafy Obscure Village in

Meru County to a Mission to Change

the World

Acclaim

Frankline is an amazing guy with a great personality; the one that you rarely find in persons in peer. His intellectual prowess combined with wit speaks volumes not only of a young man set to achieve and exceed his goals and dreams but also mentor like-minded persons to achieve same level of success. This book echo's the life of courage, determination and pursuit of excellence though from a humble beginning. A must read for young dreamers and entrepreneurs.

Paul Mwatu Director of Sales – NeoLife International Ltd East Africa

One thing I noticed with the author, Frankline Gikunda, was that he liked perfection and could beat himself to achieve it. I have worked with many technicians and engineers but haven't met many who write so eloquently. I observed he was an avid reader, quite restless and looked like someone destined for great things; this book is a proof of it."

Oliver Ogutu Founder & Director of Estream East Africa Limited

In the time that I've known the author, I've learnt that my weakness can be my greatest strength. Thank you for the inspiration; now I can face any challenge and rise to be a better person than I was before.

Karen Mumbire Director Events By Zacol, Harare – Zimbabwe

I feel greatly indebted for the privilege of reading your personal Journey. I sincerely appreciate your honesty in tackling all forms of fear and uncertainties to achieve your success. I hope the book inspires generations.

George Gakungu Muriithi, Entrepreneur and Political Strategist

Whenever I count my blessings I can't forget my smart-minded brother, Frankline. If the world could have more people like you, it would be a better place. You make a difference. A good role model to me, a mentor, leader and a hard worker. I am always praying for you and your purpose. May God keep you for this generation.

Christine Mbaga, Professional MC (MC TINA TINA) Dar es Salaam – Tanzania

Copyright © 2019 by Frankline Gikunda

All rights reserved. No part of this publication may be reproduced, stored in a retrieval system, or transmitted in any form or by any means, electronic, mechanical, photocopying, recording or otherwise, without the prior permission of the copyright owner; the author.

This book has been registered under the Kenya Copyright Board as a Copyright Work in the Literary Category number **LT-014899**

This book is based on a true story and the names of the characters have been altered to protect their identities. The views expressed might be different from those of the characters and therefore this is only but the author's perspective of his story.

All ideas shared are personal and doesn't not in any way imply the truth or expert information. Every person has different and unique experiences in life and this book does not take it into consideration. Therefore the author is not responsible for any actions taken after reading this book and anything else that happens as a result of the information offered here in.

ISBN 978-9966-131-16-4

Cover Design by: Seelex Designs Ltd

Printed by: Seelex Designs Ltd

This book is sold subject to the condition that it shall not, by way of trade or otherwise, be lent, hired out, or otherwise circulated without the authors prior consent in any form of binding or cover other than that in which it is published and without a similar condition including this condition being imposed on the subsequent purchaser.

I dedicate this Book to:

- Jesus Christ, The Lord and Savior of my life. I am nothing without you God.

- To my Dad, the late Joel Muriungi M'Rukaria for playing a big role in the conception of *"The Amerucan Dream."*

TABLE OF CONTENTS

FOREWORD 1

PROLOGUE 3

CHAPTER 1 - IT'S A BABY BOY 13

CHAPTER 2 - COMING OF AGE 35

CHAPTER 3 - WELCOME TO REAL LIFE 65

CHAPTER 4 - POWER TO READ 83

CHAPTER 5 - EARNING A LIVING 111

CHAPTER 6 - EPIPHANY 151

CHAPTER 7 – BECOMING 180

EPILOGUE 204

ACKNOWLEDGEMENTS 214

APPENDICES 219

SOCIAL MEDIA BARCODE AND QR SCANNER 221

FOREWORD

Dream is the source and hope of life. It's the oil that lubricates the purpose and meaning of life. That's why the greatest gift ever given to mankind is not the gift of sight, but the gift of having a dream. For sight is a function of the eyes; dream is a function of the heart. Its dreams - that unquenchable inspiring desire in humans - that is the engine that drives the wheels of invention, innovation, development, progress and change.

As someone who has been significantly enriched through my close association with Frankline Gikunda, I find the message in *The Amerucan Dream* remarkable, challenging and timely. This book is a life-transformative asset, not just to read but also to be used as a reference in charting our course for a better society and a richer, fulfilling life.

The Amerucan Dream seeks to inspire individuals to pursue the dream, vision, goal and plans God has placed in their hearts. It's indeed a practical tool for equipping and helping anyone to not only identify but maximize their potential as well. The book is spiritually grounded and mentally stimulating as it explores the concept that 'dream" is a powerful motivator to human activity, and that it requires the application of basic principles for effective fulfilment, which Frankline Gikunda has brilliantly endeavoured to share through the thread of his life.

The wise king of Israel, King Solomon, stated in Proverbs 29:18 that "where there is no vision (dreams) people perish." These words intrinsically capture the significant role dreams play in our individual, corporate and societal lives. There are many who have no dreams for their lives and wonder how to obtain one. There are others who have a dream but are stuck in the mud of confusion not knowing what to do next. Then there are those who had a dream but have abandoned it because of discouragement, disillusionment, failure or frustration. If you are in one of these categories, you better fasten your seatbelts, for *The Amerucan Dream* is designed to help you understand the nature of your dream, define your dream, capture or recapture a personal dream, simplify your dream, and more importantly help you put wings to your dreams as you being your dream into reality.

I congratulate my brother, friend and mentee, Frankline Gikunda on the success of this book, which is indicative of a burning desire in him to help individuals achieve their dreams, and hence live an effective and purposeful life on earth. I have no doubt that Frank's desire to impart his insight, experience and concepts to the world through this medium will bear much fruit.

I highly recommend this book to individuals who wish to discover or recapture their dreams in life.

by Douglas Waudo, Founder and CEO, LEMP –
www.lemp.co.ke

PROLOGUE

When the mention is made of Meru County in Kenya, there is one pre-dominant picture that comes with it. Especially to those not well familiar with the region. When they hear of Meru County, they think of a bushy landscape lying innocently under the foot of the ginormous Mt. Kenya. The bushy landscape in their mind is not made of ancient wild trees from the creation story. It is not even made up of the tree named after the region, the Meru Oak. It is also not made of artificial efforts of trying to reverse the deforestation in Kenya that the Late Wangari Maathai can talk about better than I can. It is not made up of eucalyptus trees planted, not to increase forest cover but to make some Kenyan Shillings when mature enough to carry 415kV of Electricity. It is not made up of annual or seasonal crops aimed at eradicating food shortage in the region, or so they think.

To them Meru County bushy landscape is made up of a very unique tree. A tree which if you owned one you qualify to be a famous Socialite in the neighboring Somalia Republic. In other words it is worth a king's ransom to our Somali Brothers. A tree that is responsible to induce insomnia to people who have to remain awake in the night; due to duty calls or to personal ambitions to beat human nature. Most drivers use it and so do our night security guards. God have mercy on us for we know how much these people mean to us. They usually have our wellbeing at hand.

This awesome specimen belonging to Kingdom Plantae is called Miraa. To most people you cannot talk about Meru County without including Miraa into the phrase. To them the words Meru and Miraa are synonymous. To them Miraa and Meru are like siblings of "Toka Nitoke". To them Meru and Miraa are like the object and its shadow. To them Meru and Miraa are like the beach and the sand: one cannot exist without the other.

Well that is what they have been made to believe or at least made self-belief. We all have preconceived notions about everything. We do not know what we do not know. Unfortunately we let ourselves swim in the ignorance and act like we know. I cannot judge their wrong perception of my home county. I remember when growing up, my primary school Geography teacher mentioned Shimo La Tewa in the coastal regions. What came to my mind was this is a place with a big pit, bigger than my rural village used as a dumpsite. And I was comfortable with my understanding, well until I later found out the truth.

So for those friends who have no idea what Meru County is, I have some good news for you! The good news is below I am showing you a picture of what is

Meru County. Let me educate the Meru misconception out of you if you will indulge me.

"And with all thy getting get understanding"
Proverbs 4:7

Seated at the chilly but fertile and evergreen highlands of Eastern Kenya is Meru County. It is the final settlement of the Ameru People after the Exodus from West Africa. Being agriculturalists by tradition it only made sense to settle in a place with the natural resources to execute the major socio-economic activity. The Meru Tribe is a fairly homogenous group comprised of nine sub-tribes, with own dialect of the Kimeru language each. The Imenti dialect is the most common, from which I come from.

The North Parts of the county habitant to the Tigania and Igembe dialect is what gives the common perception of Meru County being a big plantation of Miraa. This is the region where this stimulant crop is grown alongside other cash crops and food crops. For your information that is like one third of the Meru region. So from this point forward we can agree that Meru is NOT Miraa and Vice Versa. It would be unfair to try to describe the entire Meru County in a few sentences. It is just a large area that would need an entire book. But this short description would not be complete without diving deeper into the part of Meru that I know best. My rural village, the place I was born and raised. Sandwiched between the voluptuous hills of Meru central, Imenti South Constituency is a quiet, serene, beautiful and quite densely populated village called Rugomo in Mikumbune Location. From the geographical endowment of the area the name Mikumbune was derived. With two rivers flowing on both sides along its length, and several streams and springs in between; it is the best definition you can get for Heaven on Earth.

Close to the two rivers, Kithino and Kiuna Ndegwa, you will find the crop necessary for making your breakfast a success. From a distance you might think of it to be large well-manicured fields for grazing or whatever grass fields are used for. From a close up look, it looks like a mere shrub not more than a meter tall. Though strong and quite handsome looking with a fantastic natural smell that makes you become aware of the cause of the Late Wangari Maathai; it is easy to miss out on what it really is. It is the source of your favorite caffeinated beverage that you probably are addicted to. The tea plantations of the Mikumbune Location might be the reason you did not get a headache today for missing your caffeine dose. In between the two Rivers bordering MIkumbune you will find my neighborhood, Rugomo village. Call it the home to one of the greatest inventions in the beverage industry. Multi-million dollar businesses have been built around it. Millions of relationships created around it. Many dates led to marriage because of it. And our country Kenya put on the world map because of it.

From a distance, a visitor would think they just saw what a Miraa plant looks like. "Wow! There is Miraa", they would exclaim. "Shut up and let me take you for a tour", I would retort. For those discerned enough to hide their ignorance they would think it is one of the berry fruits sold in the organic markets for healthy conscious citizens.

Some would even take one berry and take a taste, mmmmh! That is sweet! For sure it is. But the excitement would be short lived when they find out that 95% of the berry is hard chew. Here is where I come in with no spoiler alerts to let them know that they just chewed a coffee berry. It is not poisonous to hurt them in anyway but that would make them feel stupid. And it will make a statement to them that I am the expert when it comes to my village affairs and they should follow my lead.

My folks have been coffee farmers since its introduction as a cash crop and for sure the economy of our family has been impacted by the never aging, sweet-red berried crop, coffee. It has educated some, put roofs over the heads of some and gave hope for a better tomorrow for the most. This is as close as you can get to something heaven sent. It came to lighten up our lives and bring some civilization.

Apart from the Coffee trees there is a variety of Macadamia Trees at least 100 meters apart from every direction. This is another cash crop that my village boasts of. Growing up we were told that Macadamia Nuts were used to process jet fuel in efforts to discourage us from squandering the cash crop with our little bottomless stomachs. But we all know such threats do not work so well with children. We enjoyed our fair share though in secret lest you be caught squandering the jet fuel generating cash crop that would pay your school fee for the next term.

Rugomo village boasts of itself as one of the well tree growing conscious villages in the country. Between the sub-divisions of farming plots you will find Mukima Trees ranging from a few months old to decades old. Mukima tree has been a source of decent housing in my village since the invention of the huge hand operated saw. The saw is more than 7ft tall and would be operated by two well-built men, after suspending a Mukima tree log on a 10ft high platform. One man would stand on top and the other at the bottom and the sawing begun. In a few days they will produce timber planks of different sizes that will make the structure of a decent sub-permanent house to a Rugomo resident. Up to date sawing of wood logs remains one of the greatest workmanship I have ever seen. Earlier in the 21st Century the Power saw was invented and it made the timber cutting business cheaper, quicker and more effective.

Being a cold part of the highlands, we enjoy one harvest per year of food crops like potatoes, maize and beans which are a staple in our village. However we plant numerous fruits and vegetables including: Tomatoes, Kales, Spinach, Tree tomato, Passion fruits, French beans and many others. They are consumed locally and also sold in neighboring townships. I thought I should mention this to alert you of guaranteed food security in our village. Just in case you wanted to be married in this region or may be someone you know. You can never go hungry Ha-ha!

The Agricultural practices are facilitated by the God-given rains and especially from our own ingenuity that enlighten us to tap the cool waters from River Kithino and Kiuna Ndegwa and provide every homestead with piped water. Always flowing and got our backs for all farming practices even when there are no rains. It is no doubt; we have been blessed and blessed immensely. Going hungry in our village is an abomination: not unless you are sick, mentally challenged or elderly. But even then, my people are the most generous when it comes to food as a basic necessity.

The most exciting part of spending time in my village would definitely be in the night. Of course with an exception of taking a trip outside to answer biological calls at the booth located at least 50 meters from the main house. As much as we do not have roaming wild big cats in our village it is scary for a visitor to be outside in the engulfing darkness that gives you a clue of how things were in stone-age. I have some good news; we now have electricity in our village. Thanks to the Rural Electrification Initiative by the Government of Kenya. It is better now than when I was growing up.

Back to the most exciting part of being in my village at night time. First and foremost at sunset; just as the sun is about to take a nap between the Ithangune hills which were laid down as a signage of Mt. Kenya Ahead. Birds would start echoing their joyous strains of thanksgiving to the star of the day for the great job done all day long. In a few minutes the sun will take its last winks and call it a day. The choir of the birds will retire into their humble abodes safely constructed in the strong branches of the common Meru Oak trees and a few Mukima Trees. As the birds retire they pass the button to the ever eager and always ready crickets. The crickets have a unique singing style; in our village they usually choose a duet. In a rhapsodic, harmonious orchestra they rock our night in a show that would make August Rush from the Hollywood Movie of the same name jealous. This is the best of Mother Nature's

Melodies that do not need an incentive or an award to put up a world class performance.

This experience is super therapeutic and the best way to spend a night after a busy workday. You can imagine what the dawn will be like if this is how the evening sounds like. The dawn is usually a sign of a new beginning; even the birds of the air know it. They will give you a run for your money and welcome you into the new day with triple the enthusiasm they exhibited at sunset.

Up to the age of around 10 years I thought the whole world looked and felt the same as my village because I never travelled more than 10 Kilometers from my home. You remember that time of innocent ignorance when we used to think the earth is flat and it has some 4 edges like a square? My thoughts included that everybody could talk my mother tongue and that they look like me and so were their surroundings.

Now that you have a degree of knowledge of my county, we can now get started on the real story. If you want to master it, I can arrange a tour; of course at a cost. After I got a better insight into the world outside; thanks to the black and white, 12 inch, grey Phillips TV that my dad bought back in 2000. I learnt a lot from it. For the first time I knew sunlight could be used as electricity, it was solar powered. I also felt for the first time how it feels to do school assignments under an electric bulb lightning. The biggest lessons came from watching the TV programs. It only tuned to KBC but that was enough. From my village ignorance I was transformed into knowing that there is a lot of world out there. Totally different from what I had experienced in Rugomo Village. From watching WWE Wrestling, to Tausi to The Bold and the Beautiful TV Series, I became aware of a whole new world out there. This inspired the birth of My Amerucan Dream. Do not get me wrong, I said Amerucan Dream, NOT American Dream. Ameru is the People of the Meru Tribe and Amerucan is something of or pertaining to the Ameru.

My Amerucan Dream started as a vague, childish, uninformed and Ignorant wish of things I wanted to do for my family especially my parents, my village and the new found world. I wanted to become significant and be known to those other people that I saw on my dad's little television set and interact with them. I wanted to meet them and visit their villages.

As the years went by and age kicked in, experience taught me, travelling revealed to me, interaction enlightened me and education exposed me. The Dream has gone through several changes. Changes that have refined it to the clear cut Amerucan Dream that I now Hold.

And this is the journey of my Amerucan dream.

CHAPTER 1

IT'S A BABY BOY

It is a chilly Tuesday morning; Mr. Joel Muriungi is up and about his business in his small farm. It is 11am on the dot as alerted by the news headline from his favorite KBC Swahili Radio Service. It is time to leave his 500 plants of flowering tomatoes that he has been working on since 7am. He needs to go and tend to his two dairy cattle. They need water and afterwards their midday treat of fodder. Being a hard worker and ethical human being, Joel is a very punctual and effective man in all his doings. He does it all in 30 minutes, so efficiently like he was born to take care of cattle.

Now it is thirty minutes to midday and he is starving. Being a typical Meru man he is not so quick to jump into the kitchen and fix a meal for himself. Meru culture does not advocate for their men to have so much to do in the kitchen. It is a placed preserved for our sisters and mothers. He knows he has to go in at some point but he puts it off for now. He just worked hard since the crack of dawn. A man needs a little rest after such hard labor. In the Company of his AM Tuner playing his favorite *Zilizopendwa* he will enjoy a freshly cut sugarcane from his little farm. This will give him the required energy to complete the not-so-eager-to-do task ahead; cooking.

Where is his wife? You might ask. Of course he is married. Otherwise there could not be a kitchen in his homestead in the first place. Mrs. Grace Muriungi has not been around for a few days now. Joel knows exactly where she is and the reason he really needs to make something to eat is the fact that he is going to meet her. She would be very heart broken if she realized that her beloved husband did not have his lunch because she was not around to cook for him. Being the loving man that he is Joel had to cook. Could he deceive his way out of this? No way? He knew very well if he showed up to her and lie about eating lunch he would be caught in his tracks. I do not know how she does it, but she does. Lovebirds!

Armed with this fact Joel gets his lunch ready, eats and cleans up so as not to miss the appointment he has with his beloved wife at 2:30pm. The information he wanted to get from her could be communicated over the phone but this is 1992 we are talking about. Back then some people believed that the world will come to an end in less than 8 years to come. With such ignorance no one ever bothered of the possibility of invention of the cell phone.

He puts on his bell-bottomed trouser and a matching shirt, combs his afro and slips on his dark tan Moccasin shoes and off he goes to see the love of his life that was with good news. We both know that he did not drive himself; neither did he call for an Uber. Back then there was only one way to get to his destination, walk the entire 6 Kilometers or wait to board one of the two Land Rover 110 1980 model that were plying the route. He took his chances and went for the latter.

It was on a chilly Monday morning, 20th April 1992 around 9am. It was a moment both Grace and Joel had been waiting for more than 3 quarters of a year. The time had come to reap their fruits of patience and resilience. It is a baby boy! The midwife on duty at Consolata Hospital in Nkubu, Meru announced. With all the joy she could afford at such a moment Grace took her first son in her arms and fell in love with him afresh. She could not wait to share the news with Joel her husband. But she had to wait till the next day when the visit was scheduled. The baby was too eager to meet the world and came a few hours earlier than expected.

On that Tuesday afternoon 21st April 1992, Joel was on schedule to visit and meet his newborn child. The news would be to find out if it is a baby boy or a baby girl. He received the news and as a typical Meru man it was a moment of joy and jubilation to hold his first born son in his arms. They named the child Frankline Gikunda

Muriungi, and kaboom! There I was in this beautiful world; the first born son to Mr. and Mrs. Muriungi.

My parents are quite interesting folks. My Dad Joel Muriungi was born as the first born son to my grandparents Zaverio M'Rukaria and Juliet Karambu. He landed on this planet just a few days before Kenya celebrated its first *Jahmuri* day on 9th December 1963. My dad is an *Uhuru* kid and boasts an age equivalent to that of The Republic of Kenya. He was to be the first born among 6 brothers and 1 sister.

Being a first born he had to man up quickly to handle the responsibility of helping my grandparents in taking care of my uncles and aunt. I am convinced some of his great leadership skills were developed at this tender age. All his workmanship and drive for serving and helping out must have been nurtured at this level. Of course not consciously but as the duty demanded.

My grandparents were informed of the benefits of education. My grandpa had some under his collar but he opted out early to pursue his extravagant politics. This did not last long, he had found a hobby in sampling alcoholic drinks and this was weighing down on him and threatening to take him hostage. Your guess is as good as mine; he became an alcoholic in the long term.

This was not a great experience especially for my dad. During coffee bonus pay days, dad had to go pick him from a local joint and take him home, number one, to make sure he brings some money back home and number two, for his safety. This was something my dad got accustomed to in his teenage and young adulthood.

Irrespective of his drinking habits, my grandpa was very strict on education and though in hardships, he made sure everyone went to school. For my dad, he was a bright one, passed his primary school examination, CPE and was admitted to one of the good schools in the district; Nkuene Boys High School. He passed well and got a direct admission to Murang'a Teachers College for his O Level education

Here comes the bad news. He needed Ksh. 1000 for the admission to the teachers college. My grandpa did not have the money for that. Besides according to him, my dad had achieved something his siblings had not yet achieved. In other words he was done with him and onto the rest. He had a decision to make, to be angry at his father or to suck it up, put on some farming cape and help him in the farm. Being the awesome man that he is, he chose the latter.

He had a plan to help grandpa in farming so that his siblings could go through school and also save up to pay for his tuition at the teachers college. But as the days went by, he become the main person responsible for the rest of his siblings and his disengagement in the farm, which was mainly coffee farming, would mean that his siblings would not be able to complete school. For the obvious reason, there would not be enough cash flow to take care of their education and upkeep. He had a decision to make, to give up on his future and take care of his siblings or forget them and pursue his dreams.

One of the things I admire in this great son of God is his giving heart. He sacrifices a lot so that someone can benefit even when it would mean great inconvenience for him. So he gave up on his dreams and became a full time farmer for the sake of everyone's sake and keep tables spinning in the Rukaria's homestead. This says a lot about a man. So believe me when I say God gave me the best dad in the world. I have learnt a lot from his personal story and picked some of the great traits he developed from such an upbringing. He is just the type of man you want to respect and salute.

Meet my Mum Grace Muriungi. She was born in 1973 as the 4th born in a family of 5. A tall Amerucan lady, midnight black hair that stays natural, dark chocolate glossy skin, and big smile complimented by pearl white teeth to top it all. She has joyous a personality and is a great listener too. Rarely will you catch her complaining; she is solution oriented and focused on the bright side of things. She is a great cook who can make something tasty from anything. Up to date I marvel how she always nails it. She is the only person I know who can cook tasty *sukumawiki* without tomatoes. Am not saying that she is world class; she does not even know what lasagna is but she knows her stuff.

I know she is a bright lady though she did not make it far in the school system. Class 7 was the best her parents could do. I know if she got an opportunity she could have done great and I know she could have been a fashion designer or something close to that. This woman has an eye for fashion and she knows how to invent looks. I am convinced that my artist side was gotten from my mum. I remember when growing up when she used to knit matching sweaters for me and my siblings. She is good with her hands. Give her a yarn, a pair of knitting needles or a crochet hook and she will make whatever you can describe to her. She is that good with her needles.

If you wanted to know what colors would match with what, ask her. If you want to know what kind of shoes to wear or not to wear with a certain outfit, ask her. If you want to look unique and artistic, ask her. And all these gets me wondering; if she can do all these with little or no education in the sector, what would she do if she got her fair share of 8.4.4 system. Only God knows. I am reminded of the Swahili proverb, "*Penye miti hapana wajenzi.*"

Mum has been at my dad's side for as long as I can remember. She is his personal assistant, his second in command in everything. She knows as much about farming as my dad knows. During harvest she is the sales and marketing manager with an exception of coffee that Dad cannot delegate to anyone. I remember when growing up she would wake up at the crack of dawn put a sack of kales or whole bunch of banana or a sack of yams on her back, walk for 6 kilometers to the nearest township of Nkubu to make her sale. I remember the market days well, it was on Tuesdays, Thursdays and Saturdays. I remember them well because anytime my mum went to the *soko*; she would bring us bread and sweets. And on most occasions we ate a special meal like rice, taking a break from the staple; *githeri, ugali* and *mukimo*.

"Whatever your hand finds to do, do it with all your might, for in the realm of the dead, where you are going, there is neither working, nor planning nor knowledge nor wisdom" Ecclesiastes 9:10 [NIV]

To these great humble people I was born. Being the first born son they definitely had great hopes for me just like it is in most African cultures. The first male child is usually looked up to, to take up some leadership in the family especially in setting a good example for the siblings. On top of this I was the first Male child to be named after my grandpa. So it meant I was not only tasked on setting a good example to my siblings but also my cousins. In Amerucan, being the first to be named after your grandpa puts you automatically in a leadership position.

My second name Gikunda, which in Kimeru means someone who drinks, was inspired by grandpa. Remember I told you that he had an appetite for alcoholic drinks. The guy had a brewery in his farm. It was a norm to make tradition brews called *kithiri or muratina*, also common among the kikuyu and sugarcane was the main ingredient. It involved having special equipment for extracting sugarcane juice. With dried *muratina* tree fruits split into half and set in a special pot called *kithiri*, the juice was poured in. Then this mixture was fermented. In 36 hours or less, it would be tasty alcoholic beverage that graced most ceremonies. I wonder where this tradition disappeared too.

It was obvious for me to get this name considering the craft grandpa had developed and lead for most of his energetic years. Up until to date grandma does not believe that I shall forever stay away from falling into grandpas footsteps. Of course I have and I will continue to emulate the great things about him. My grandma reckons him as the most handsome man in the world. I tend to agree with her, he brought the gene of tall, dark and handsome into the bloodline. Grandma, though short, the person I recognize to have the tallest memory and longest wisdom. She is quite talkative; I think that is where I got my chatterbox qualities. Always full of stories; from the stories of the last *MauMau* fighters to how she met the flame of her heart to how she raised my dad to her 7th child. She enjoys feeding people too. If you spend a day with her, be sure you will be reminded to eat something at least once per hour. She has a PHD in Grand-mother-hood, she is the best.

Being raised in such an environment where my parents had a little taste of the education system, it was expected to walk the 8.4.4 System way. My parents had the drive to provide us with the education they got too little of because of unavoidable circumstances. Their fears were the inability to provide us with sufficient education. They look up to us to put their name in the map, a thing they could not do considering their backgrounds. They were committed and still are to make sure I got the basic needs so that I would never use an empty stomach or unclothed body as a scapegoat not to pass my exams. I applaud my parents for I do not recall a single day that I went to bed hungry. With an exception of those days I got fed up of eating *Githeri* or I was mad at my mum for punishing me after some boyish mischief. Those were the times I refused to eat as a way to get back at my mum. But she has seen it all; she knew I would wake up the next morning turning things inside out as I look for my share of last night's meal.

They kept me out of loads of chores at home to a point that grandma and other relatives started complaining. In their understanding, any boy child should have the skills to milk cows as soon as their little hands can squeeze milk out of a cow's udder. But not my parents they wanted to make sure we had ample time to study, play and do all things that children do to be themselves; children. This alone qualifies my parents to have a Nobel Prize in parenthood. However it was not easy being their child. Back then I did not understand them but now I do. We always had a hard time when I wanted a new shoe or clothing that I thought would make me cool. It would drive me nuts when I approached my mum with suggestion and get a reply that went in the lines of, I do not have any money, go and ask your dad. My dad was the tough one, telling him something mum was not supportive of would be as useless as washing chickens legs (Ameru Proverb)

Now I understand why they did that, they had their priorities and it was for my best interest.

"Since the child knew his parents would give in, he tried the same trick again and again." Jackie Chan

The baby boy was growing up quick and it came time to start going to school. I remember this day so clearly like it was yesterday. It was a sunny but somewhat chilly morning of January 1997 when I got enrolled to Mikumbune Nursery School, within the compound of Mikumbune Primary School. I was 4 years and 8 months old but tall enough to reach my left ear with my right hand over my head which was the qualification to join nursery school. I do not know where these orthodox methods came from but I was glad they favored me. Back then joining nursery school was like trying out for military recruitment where you are told to come back next year if you did not qualify. Those unfortunate enough to have shorter hands were sent back home for another whole year. Some were even older than I was. I know it is unfair but those were the rules.

My first day at school was about touching my left ear with my right hand and being told which classroom I would come into the next day. The second day was more interesting. Of course I cried after my mum left me in the midst of new little faces that gave me a look suggesting that they would make a hell out of my day. Give me a break, I came here to learn how to read and probably go teach my grandma; my best friend. Of course they could not hear my thoughts and I later came to learn that they were as scared of me I was of them. The teacher, Madam Eunice came in and started to arrange us in a class format, urging others to stop crying and helping others sit in their little wooden desks. We all had a little note book that was not more than 32 pages and a pencil that had a rubber on one end. It was a safety requirement that no child was to have a pencil sharpener; that duty was left to Madam Eunice our teacher and mother for the best part of the weekdays for the rest of the year.

Up to date I marvel at how early childhood development personnel can manage to deal with noisy, crying and stubborn little humans bringing order and collaboration. The memories of the entire year in nursery school is not so clear in my head but I remember by the end of it I could do my ABCDEF... forward and backward, I could read simple English words and draw a few items. I also had realized that 1+1=2 not 11. Another thing I remember was our playtime in school which was more invested into than being in class. We had developed a skill to hunt beetles from cow dung. Of course this was a boy's only thing with one or two girls who liked hanging out with the men.

We made these Beetles our pets and we even named them. What was most clever is that we had figured the right food to feed them with. Of course their lifespan in our action filled lives was short, but there were always new hunting grounds for more beetles, bigger and even tougher to keep up with us. The most favorite was a breed that had a rhinoceros kind of a horn. Bagging this Rhinoceros beetle was the ultimate goal to the hunting teams. We would later meet and compare who had what and see who did well. Thanks to being born in the village, our nursery school year was fun. I know some people who are scared of cockroaches; I wonder what they could have done in my situation. Those little animals were all the toys and pets given to us by life. This was before Disney world became known so we did not know about cartoon super heroes that could double down as toys. And it was known not in our village.

But you do not know what you do not know, we were happy with our beetles and cars we made from plastic container lids; talk of creativity. I am a fan of technology but think it is also making our children less creative. Some corporate is dictating to a child how he/she should grow and that is quite limiting. Especially at this age when someone is discovering what the world is about. Anyway that is a topic for another day.

This baby boy just passed his test to join Class One in January 1998, Yaaay! First victory! That is besides succeeding to reach my ear over my head with the opposite hand. At this point I had developed some sizeable level of confidence and I was already proud of what I was becoming. The System was not so bad after all, it was equipping well so I liked it. I looked forward to learning bigger stuff that Class one had to bring. Bring it on!

While class one was nothing much as I expected. I thought the long breaks and the half day in school would remain. I thought the play time with clay; and I mean real clay gotten from River *Kithino*, would remain. Things were a little more grown up here. We got introduced to caning as a means of punishment when we did wrong. Something like incorrect answer to a question that you voluntarily lifted up your hand to answer, would earn you a few strokes of the Bamboo stick cane. That was the learning environment I went through. Thinking about now, it is either we were too stupid and we needed some pain inflicted into us to divorce the village ignorance or our teachers did not know how to motivate 6 year olds to learn.

One thing I do not understand up to date is the reason why they included mother tongue as a subject in the lower primary classes. This did more damage than good because it gave our teachers the freedom to teach us other subjects in Kimeru. Imagine being taught English Language in Kimeru! No wonder most of us have a hard time getting rid of our Kimeru accent. This is not an excuse but bear with me for a moment; number one, you were taught your mother tongue as a subject for 3 years, and then number two your teachers used your mother tongue to teach everything else. What do you expect? Research has it that we are a result of the things we learnt from ages 0 -7. This is the best time to teach a child different languages, when they are still in the formation stage of building their belief system. This is not the time to limit them and dictate a disempowering way of doing things.

Enough with the ranting, I just had to get it off my chest. The three years I spent in lower primary were quite confusing. I did not know what I was good at. When most kids could brag about being good in Mathematics or Science or Art & Craft, I did not relate to any. I liked science but I was but an average performer in everything. I remember my talks with my mum in her little smoke filled kitchen while waiting for supper. I would express my frustrations and she would reassure me that I had nothing to worry about. That I had a long way to go and I would figure things out with time. And she uplifted my spirits by stating I will become a great scientist because I loved science. She gave hope and encouragement to the little me. She gave me hope when it really mattered. Even those times when I scored my mathematics below the pass mark, she would still encourage me. I do not remember my mum ever scolding me for poor performance in school. Much less I can say about my dad. He is the results oriented kind of a person.

School got more interesting when I got to Upper primary. This is the time we started learning geography and I got a chance to learn about the world outside my village. The exams were also friendlier with the multiple choices and the teachers were more sensitive to the language they used.

At this point it was also declared a crime to be found speaking *Kimeru* in the school compound. They should have done this in class one, not now! I thought. There was a small wooden plank that used to be passed around to those found breaking the law. At the end of the day, the class teacher would come and collect the names of those found guilty of propagating the insignificant language in the school compound for punishment. This kept us on track to speak in English or Swahili. Most of the time our English was broken and our Swahili was a blend of a little Swahili and handful of Kimeru. You could hear the class monitor yell, *"stop beating noise!"* (stop making noise) in efforts to call the class to order.

"A man's grammar, like Ceaser's wife, should not only be pure, but above suspicion of impurity." – Edgar Allan Poe

---

Then the year 2002 happened. His Excellency Mwai Kibaki was elected as the POROK; President of the Republic of Kenya. He had promised to bring free primary education. This was a great moment for us in Mikumbune Primary School. It meant enough text books, sufficient exercise books and better classrooms and facilities. All we had to do was to show up and sit in the class. Books were provided, branded and of good quality. Parents were only left with the responsibilities of buying uniform and feeding us. We could now compete with those in private schools as we had more text books to read and catch up with them. Before this, in most cases you would find only one copy of the book, reserved for the teacher. We therefore had to copy our assignments from the blackboards. But thanks to this new government our hope was elevated.

2002 remains a great landmark in my life because apart from the free primary education, two more things happened. I was in Class 5 and now I had a better understanding of things. I had finally made it through catechism class after flanking around 3 times. It was during the August holiday, precisely the first week. In the village, play time was as important as eating time. Having grown up, we had graduated from hunting beetles and riding tin lids toys. We now had the skills to manufacture a football from polythene paper and nylon threads. We had the skills to curve toys from wood; the favorite being a car model that had 4 wheels and we would ride them with a long stick that would rest on the shoulders with a cross bar that was used as the steering. This took a lot of workmanship and willingness to work with a sharp *panga*.

On this day I had resolved to make my car that would rock my August holiday. So I searched for the right wood; perfectly round, 4 inch thick Jacaranda tree log for wheels. Jacaranda tree was the easiest to work with. It has uniform thread and does not crack after drying. I went to work; of course my mum was around and she advised strongly not to go through with it as I ran a risk to injure myself. She definitely underestimated my determination to make myself a toy. I sneaked from her vicinity and continued to work on my brand new toy.

Little did I know what I was to encounter; in a moment I would come face to face with the meaning of the Swahili proverb, "Asiye sikia la mkuu huvunjika guu." As I was shaping my 3rd wheel into a uniform 1 inch tall cylinder, the dreaded happened. My left hand pinky finger was caught between the curving surface and the blade of the *panga* I was using. At first I did not feel any pain. I even lifted the *panga* to continue putting my wheel into shape, this time with my finger tucked away from the harm's way. This is when I realized what had happened and I was already bleeding profusely. I said I would hide my accident from my mum. I was to nurse my wound and keep it undercover, or so I thought.

Prior to my car toy designing escapades I had squeezed one meter of sugarcane out of its delicious juice. So my blood sugar was high and those that know with this situation it takes time for blood to clot. So the bleeding did not stop as quick as I thought it would and I started getting scared. I feared dying and at that moment I swallowed my pride and ran to mama for help. After examining my pinky she diagnosed that it was a deep cut and I had cut a blood vessel. This needs to be taken to a clinic for further dressing, she resolved. She used some herbs to slow down the bleeding, changed into a decent dress and we were on our way to the nearest clinic more than 3 kilometers away.

It is at the clinic that I learned that I had almost chopped off the tip of my pinky finger. The nurse did the proper dressing and said that the tip would reattach to the finger as the healing takes place. We went home; the painkillers proved not to be effective. The pain was unbearable. Plus a throbbing feeling that felt like my heart had migrated to my left hand. During all these we did not talk much with mama but I knew she was mad at me. This was the worst that life could get to any human being, regardless of age, I thought.

Two days after my accident, I went to be dressed by my uncle who was a student in a nursing school. He had just gotten home after completing his studies. I thought things were getting better with time but my uncle, who was now my doctor; had some news. My finger was not healing as expecting. The cut piece did not have blood supply and was bringing infection to the wound. They did not ask me; him and my parents but they said the best way out was to remove the entire tip off my finger. If I ever wanted a healthy pinky finger, this was the prize. I surely paid it with pain that remains fresh in my pinky finger. As I am typing this I see it shy of and tuck itself away from the rest of the fingers. Fingers have memories, I have learned that.

After that painful ordeal, the healing continued well with daily appointments with my uncle. He was kind to me and he usually gave me some painkillers before nursing my wound. He remains to be one of the kindest people I know to date. God Bless Uncle Patrick.

My 2002 August holiday continued. I had not seen my best days yet. For the first time in my life I was to leave my home county and cross two more counties to visit my aunt in Mwea, Kirinyaga County. For the first time I would travel more than 10 Kilometers from my village. For the first time I would see the world outside my village with my own eyes. I was still nursing my pinky but that was not to stop me from enjoying this trip. I had travelled before, but to my mum's home place less than 15 kilometers from my village. That is the furthest I had gone. A total village boy I was.

My trip to my Aunts in Mwea; the home of Kenyan *Pishori rice*, was an eye opener to me. I saw the world in a totally new light. It was like I had worn a brand new pair of eyes. For the first I was in an environment where children knew the cartoon network characters by name, traits, looks, and circumstances. I met children who did not have to cut off their pinky fingers to get toys. I met children who had toy cars that moved without being pushed. I met children who had superhero dolls. I met children who could speak fluent Swahili and some nice English that got my village self-esteem below the zero level.

Yes I was challenged; but thanks to the child I was, I was not discouraged. I was determined to learn what they knew. I spent time asking questions. I was taught how to operate a TV remote and for the first I watched a movie from a video cassette. It was a Mr. Bean Movie. I was so happy that I would have a lot of experiences to share with my fellow village boys when the schools opened. I even fantasized how I would write an awesome composition for my English class titled, MY AUGUST HOLIDAY.

"Progress is impossible without change, and those who cannot change their minds cannot change anything." – George Bernard Shaw

---

CHAPTER 2

COMING OF AGE

It was in November 2005, the second week. Here comes the final event of my primary school education. I was a teenager now. A lot had happened since the August holiday of 2002. I gotten used to barely making it to the pass mark of Mathematics subject. Science still remained my favorite subject and somehow I liked writing Compositions for my English class.

I would really like to end my primary school story without any more unpleasant events. But my conscience will not let me. Growing up; especially through the primary school, I had a great weakness that I do not understand up to date. I was the kind of boy who did not take criticism or any kind of humiliation kindly. If I had the physical capacity I could have reacted physically. But I was short and skinny. My only defense was to give in to the emotions and cry it out. Some bullies made it a routine to switch my crying on by making fun of me. I was stuck into this. I tried to act strong, wear a Kevlar around my emotions and become bullet proof and I failed terribly. I was a cry baby and everyone knew it. Even the friends I had used it occasionally for entertainment; so evil but they did not know better.

One of my biggest dreams was to grow out of it. To reach that level that I am bullet proof of people's opinion about me. I knew what they thought or said just for the sake of it was not true. It was not my reality. But since I was not the expressive person, the only way I let off the frustration was to cry it out. I felt imprisoned for not being able to stand up for myself in front of my critics. I was dying inside because I could not voice my feelings or at least gain the courage to speak up for myself. I wished to have the right thing to say at the right time to neutralize my tormentors. I wished to learn how to express myself and prove them wrong. I just wanted to identify my voice and speak up for myself when it mattered most.

It was quite a serious situation because it affected how I asked for what I needed from my parents. If I really needed something all I could do was state it, but I did not have the convincing power to motivate them to give it up. A few times I found myself crying; I think I was crying so that my parents could have pity on me and do what I asked. But the more I did it the more they got frustrated with this teenager son who was not showing any signs of growing up to the macho man that our culture expects. Part of it was because my parents were of modest means but all said and done, they knew I should have acted differently. Crying was my means of communication and I did not like it at all.

All through the primary school I was trying to find my voice; to find my unique gift. I was not the best in the class; I was not the best in any sport. I actually played no sport at all. My parents were not supportive of it and I also did not resonate with any. I could not draw. I could make jokes. I could not write great compositions that attracted the attention of all teachers in the staffroom. I was just an underdog. The only reason I was known was that my dad was the Chairperson at my church and also in the schools board of governors. In class 8, I tried to join the gymnastics team. It was coached by the schools head teacher. I was not good at it but I was determined to make it to the team that goes for the competitions. All was well until my dad through the head teacher got me off the team. It was said that I did not have what it takes to make the team. And I was back to my lack of identity.

The biggest hope I had in my life was that my mum used to believe in me so much that I wondered if she was real. I kept my eyes on the education ball because that is the only thing I could say I can do even though at an average level. Another hope I had was that I would grow tall and when I join secondary school I would play basketball. In my village basketball was not invented yet. I had to wait for high school. I knew Michael Jordan and Chicago Bulls and I wanted to be like him. Those born in my time can remember the green polythene bags that had a picture of MJ and Chicago bulls with the number 23 on his jersey. That is how I met MJ. I did not Google him.

Let us go back to November 2005. It was on Monday and it was time for rehearsal to prep for our KCPE exams. In the next three days, the first 8 years of the 8.4.4 system would be history. We were psyched up because in a months' time we would go through the rite of passage that would make a man out of the boys we were. In the Meru culture this is a main event to a boy child's life. It is a mark into adulthood and also a sign of maturity and coming of age. For mine it came after Christmas of 2005 when the KCPE results came out. In our village once you go through the rite of passage you cannot go back to primary school. My parents wanted to make sure that I had secured a good score to get me into a decent High school; failure to which I was expected to retake class 8.

"May your Choices reflect your hopes, not your fears." – Nelson Mandela

---

On Saturday 14th January 2006 very early in the morning I was up getting ready to report to St. Pius X Seminary in *Nkubu*, Meru County. The school is located 6 kilometers east of my village. It is in the township where my mum used to go to sell the farm produce. It is a walking distance; we had severally walked to and from Nkubu town. But this was a special day. And we had the main road reconstructed from all-weather to tarmac. Public transport had gotten easier for our location.

I was accompanied by my dad. Being quite a time keeper we were at St. Pius X Seminary by 8am and I was admitted to the form one class of 2006 as the second person. I remember very well, I was Admission number 3502, after the first 3501. I was to spend the rest of the day exploring this new environment and getting myself new friends. I had lots of hopes for my time in high school. Shyness and my village low self-esteem were not welcome here. It was time to step out of my comfort zone and grow. It was time to own my life and make friends from a better background than I had. It was time to get exposed to new people and ways of thinking and doing. I was willing to learn.

The first thing I wanted to confirm availability of was the basketball court. From this concrete floor I was to learn the skills that made Michael Jordan a star that he came to be; to the extent of being known by a village boy swimming in obscurity. I knew there were older boys in this institution that would train the village out of me and the basketball basics into me. I felt at home with this fact in mind. I could not wait to touch that orange basketball. It would be my first time not only to hold a basketball but also to meet it face to face. The closest I ever came close to it was through my dad's black and white TV and a few newspapers. I knew its color from the latter.

St. Pius Seminary was a state of the art institution in comparison to what I was exposed to so far. Storeyed buildings that were literary inter-joined to bring every aspect of the school in one location. The administration block, classes, dormitories, the Chapel and the dining room were all in a loop. Some of the buildings dated back to 1956 when the school was started by missionaries. It was nice to be a part of a school that was older than our nation.

For the first time in my life I used staircases. In St. Pius X Seminary stair cases were a means of transport; from class to the dormitories, from the dining room to the class. This was definitely a new world to me. Thanks to my quick adaptability I did not look out of place. I behaved like everything was a normal thing from where I come from. Of course we do have tens of flights of stairs in our *Mukima* timber house.

Being a student at *'Semo'*, as we used to call our school, was special. Though for a teenager it felt like a torture and tyrannical way of doing things. I will explain why. For the first time, I was required to pray at least 4 times a day. An early morning Eucharistic celebration, midday prayers before lunch, evening prayers before supper and night prayers before going to bed. At this age this would have been a perfect plan. We are now spiritually mature and we understand the purpose of having time to pray. But not in 2006; this was the closest one could ever get to being imprisoned. God forgive my ignorant and rebellious teenage mindset.

My High-school life was full of intrigues and learning curves. I mainly associated myself with the guys from the big cities and those who were in boarding and/or private primary schools. They seemed to have a better understanding of how the world works more than my fellow villagers and public primary school grads. They knew what movies were a must watch, which song is on the top 10 hit list and they seemed to have had classes to memorize all the trendy songs. They knew which artist recorded what song and they could even name the record label. Before then I thought Calif is a village in Nairobi; when Juacali used to say in his music, California *'vitu vizuri'* I thought he was talking about his village. I was told by my out-of-the-heart of Nairobi friend that it was a record label. Oh! I was in for a lot of learning, more than I anticipated.

My first day in class; Form 1B, one of the 3 streams of my former high school, was kind of the most embarrassing. Our class Teacher Mr. Mithika came to class to get everyone introduced and as the captain of the ship, to give a notice how he would like to sail the ship. As the students, we were required to stand up, say your name, your former primary school and where it is located and then what you scored in the KCPE exam. Oh Boy! A public speaking gig at this stage is the last thing I was hoping for. That was too much information to give with my broken-*Kimeru* influenced English and a village boy confidence. At this point a toddler born in the civilization of a city had more confidence in its pinky finger than I could amass in my whole body. I knew I was a speaker but this was like an international stage to me. For the first time I would be speaking to a group of people who were not purely of Ameru Tribe. The first time I spoke in front a group of people, it was during my catechism test and I froze, resulting to a fail. The second was during a cultural festival at church, we were presenting a memory verse and again I froze.

My history with speaking in front of people said that I was not cut out for it. I am the guy who had to retake catechism classes 3 times just because I could not present myself during testing. "Here we go again", I heard a voice in my head tell me, time to make fool of you one more time. But I was determined to set off on a good course in this new environment. I took some deep breaths, wore my big handsome smile and with all the charisma that I could afford, I said my name, even managed to pull off a joke about my primary school and my village and by the time I was done at least everyone in the class was smiling if not laughing. First public victory in high school, it deserved a happy dance only that I did not have one.

After this first day in class I was both encouraged and discouraged. I was encouraged because I did well speaking in front of the class. I was discouraged because I learnt that I was one of the few people who had lower scores in the final primary school exam. The latter meant to me that I will always be the last in the class and I would never catch up with the others who were in private schools. I am a competitive person; in this setting the odds were stacked against me. But I was open-minded; I let it be a time-will-tell thing and moved on.

A few months later we would be doing our first test to mark the end of our first term in secondary school. By this time I had learnt a lot. From what biology is to what chemistry is, to why mathematics is the villain to our hero journeys; to what physics says about matter and so many other things that left me wondering if Frankline the son of Joel would ever find real life application of the stuff.

So we did the test. Your guess is as good as mine; of course I did better than I expected. I even managed to get one of the highest scores in mathematics that would hold a significant position in my entire high school education. That is a story for another day. I managed to get position 17 out of close to 100 students. This was a happy dance moment for me. High school was treating me well and now I started dreaming bigger dreams.

Talking of big dreams; I liked the lifestyle of our fellow students who were prefects and captains of different departments in school. They were almost free from any sort of punishment especially due to lateness. They could come to class a few minutes later and just get away with it. They never did things in a hurry. They were never assigned duties to do cleaning of the school; they supervised. They lived a big life according to the standards of the high school environment. I hated the life I led and I also longed to get the freedom that they had. I made it a goal to become a captain in any way possible.

The first step was to identify what made people get picked as prefects and captains. I realized number one item of consideration was discipline. Good news for me, I was well behaved, I stood a chance. The second thing was academic excellence. To me this was a work in progress but I knew I could make it. No one made to captain status without getting to Form 2. I had enough time to work on my grades. The third thing was to make known your leadership skills by getting known by the relevant teachers and the high ranking student leadership. Obscurity was not an option in this race. I did everything possible for them to know who I was; from our class prefect, to the class teacher, to the school captain to the school principal.

In my efforts to show myself cool and in my struggle to get the village out of me I did a few mistakes. The most memorable was something that happened in the second term of first year. My fellow students from the city, Nairobi, seem to know every musician that ever passed the face of the world starting with King David up to date. To me this was an ability that I would greatly love to be recognized for. Knowing what song was sung by whom, under what recording label and the inspiration that brought the song. This was cool stuff.

With all my village-ness I stumbled upon a few names of the known artist of that. If my memory serves well it was Deux Vultures and Kleptomaniax. To show how cool I was I took a red ink pen and typed the names on the color of my uniform so that everybody would see. See they did. At the top of the world I felt; but short lived. It started with the school captain, who I had already befriended, ordering me to go change into a clean shirt. No sooner had I heeded to the order than I met the teacher on duty. This was to be a tougher punishment. I get me a few strokes from a bamboo cane in the hands of the fierce and well-built Mr. Kirimi.

From this moment I came to realization that I have nothing to prove. I found out anytime you try to prove something it means that it is not in you; I found out that it shows lack of authenticity. It also comes back to you and stabs you in the back making a fool out of you. Lesson learnt, let us move on.

The rest of the year in form one was filled with many learning opportunities. Some which were to shape my life up to date. I remember this day very well like if it was my previous birthday. I was paying a visit to my friend from the village in their dormitory. At St. Pius we were assigned dormitories according to your academic year. He was in Form 4, so I was in the form 4 dormitory. We had a moment of chit chat in mother tongue in low tones so that no one in the authorities, (read prefects) could hear. It was a therapeutic moment because for once my vocal chords were producing familiar sounds. Those that I did not struggle to voice out.

It was time to leave and I had to bid him goodnight. Then this happened. I do not know if it was default or if it was the sudden change from Kimeru to a different language that had strict rules on pronunciation. This is what I said, *"Acha niende nikarare..."* I do not remember the rest of the statement. For the sake of this story, the above phrase is good enough. What I meant was in Swahili, *"naenda kulala…"* meaning it was time to go and sleep.

Unfortunately my bad pronunciation fell on the wrong ears and I was made to pay for it with public humiliation. One of the schools bullies happened to be around and heard my *Kimeru* accent influenced Swahili statement. He burst into one of the most ridicule filled laughter and made sure that everyone around knew the source of his gigantic laughter. For a moment I was the laughing stock for something I did unconsciously. My self-esteem was held ransom for things that I had no control over. I did not choose to be born a Meru and you are damn right, I was not taught pronunciation in my early childhood development education. The latter was absent.

Yes it was a humiliating moment in my life and I remember asking God. Do I have to carry this baggage with me for the rest of my life? Can I get better? I know to some, you might ask; what is the big deal? Why not accept it and move on? That was not an option for me. At that point in time I was all about learning and growth. So settling was just not an option. This is what I did. From that moment henceforth, I decided to focus on the words coming out of my mouth. I did it consciously for quite some time until it became like second nature. Every now and then my tongue would slip to pronouncing what comes easily to it but I was not worried because I saw improvement. I knew I was getting better and that is what mattered most.

Up to date I have those once in a while slip of the tongue but I can confidently say that my *Kimeru* accent influenced speech has greatly improved. I now know better and I accept my roots and worry less about what people say or do not say about my speech but I thank God this happened. It was a great lesson that I have used to make several other improvements in my life. This was my first breakthrough in self-development; which later came to be my passion.

Thinking about it now, I kind of get mad at my fellow Kenyans for alienating our fellow countrymen for their accents. After being exposed I realized the French have an accent that affects their English, so do the Germans, the Russians, Spanish, Chinese and all people worldwide who do not use English as their first language. But we consider their accents cool; while we perceive ours as a disability. This is so sad and it is my prayer that we all recognize that we have the right to be ourselves just like everyone else around the world.

"Praying doesn't mean kneeling down"
an Amerucan Proverb

This proverb from my people simply means a prayer is not identified by consciously kneeling down and getting to it. It means the words we utter with our mouths are like prayers. It means what we pronounce, we produce. It means what we affirm, we confirm. That is why in the Bible we are told that the power of life and death are in the tongue.

I do not remember ever seriously praying for a chance to become a prefect or a captain. It was in form 2 when we now had a chance to be selected to captain certain departments in school. I remember I was just introduced to some of the most interesting topics in chemistry and I was really becoming good at it. The periodic table! Rings a bell? It was the easiest thing I could ever do in school. My chemistry teacher Mr. Mithika became a great friend since I quickly resonated with what he was trying to teach in class. I was good at writing the chemical equations and balancing them without cutting a sweat. I could easily fill the periodic table with the first twenty elements on the basis of energy levels and atomic number. During practical lessons at the laboratory I also did well.

It was not a surprise I came out as the best student in chemistry in the end of first term examination. I scored a clean A and I was at the top of the world. To whom who has, more shall be added to them; goes my favorite book. The coming term I was honored with an opportunity to be the captain heading the schools laboratories. #dreams come true. #prayers answered. My responsibility was to make sure that the labs were well cleaned, helping the lab technician schedule for practical, to raise any complaint from students about their experience in lab: especially the supplies of material needed for learning. My life was not going to be the same again from now hence forth. I am now a captain and I did not intend to lose the title; may be a promotion to a better position.

"To lead an orchestra you must turn your back on the crowd." – Aristotle

---

High school was the best thing that happened to me. I am sure I am a better person now as a result of the experiences I went through at that point in time. Overall I was a disciplined teen. I never got into trouble because of the latter, with the exception of noise making. I like to talk, I like conversations, I like telling stories as well as listening to them. This was the greatest of character flaws that always got me into the wrong side of the school rules. But the good news for me was I was in a class that was well known for its inability to maintain graveyard silence as was required during preps. It served me since we were approached as a class but not an individual. Of course you can bet that I was a main character in the noise making cartel.

I remember while in Form 3, stream A, class of 2008, we had close to 70% of the student leadership in our class. This was the toughest times for the teachers on duty. Sometimes they had to camp in our class to at least regulate the noise making. We were always a topic of discussion during school assemblies. Thank God we had grades that washed our noise making sin away. That is why we got so many captains in one class in the first place.

Apart from the noise making and the many captains, we also had the leadership of almost every student organization and clubs represented in our class. During the club functions it was obvious to find close to three quarter of the class absent. Talk of the best dancers, show stoppers and MCs; they mostly came from our class. I think our good grades were as a result of the play-hard-and-grades-will-follow culture we had developed.

We used to be known in the region as the people who rock club functions especially in the schools entertaining our sisters. My classmates literally used their waking time strategizing how to make the next function better than the rest. How they would etch their names in the hearts of the visiting girl schools. How they would beat the competition; read boys school. If not strategizing about functions, moments were spent discussing dada-issues. Everyone has a concern about the opposite sex; tips, advice and counsel from the smooth operators in the class was highly sought. Love letters would be written after forming a board of advisors and consultants. They would offer the best approach to write for the situation; love quotes would be coined, RnB songs dedicated, best handwriting would be used to type the important document. Last but not the least a calligrapher would type the address on the envelope in an art that would melt a female heart even before opening the contents inside. We did not care about authenticity, what mattered was creating a lasting impression.

Things were going well. So well, we were winning in the class and socially we were putting our schools name on the map. The attitude that people used to have about our school was changing and changing fast. Being a Catholic school; a seminary in that matter, most people thought we were leading some kind of religious lifestyle that made us different from other schools. Some thought we were all headed to religious careers like missionaries, priests and monks. But we were committed to help the society transform their perspective by renewing their point of view about us.

It was during the wave of dancing crews that rocked our local music videos, TVs and concerts. We were not left behind; we had at least two terrific dance crews: The Talibans and Gutsy Dancers. I do not know why the former used the terror associated name but it worked. They terrorized the competition on the dance floor and they were fierce. They carried our fame to the next level: we were setting standards of how high school club functions should be done and we were winning.

Then something happened. Up until this moment we did our thing but still maintained the high discipline that our school was credited for. We never got into any trouble by taking things too far with competition (read the boys schools). It is something that started as a mere effort to appear on the well-known high school magazine, The Insider. I do not know if it exists up to date but it was such thing back in our days.

A few of our school mates wrote an article of some kind to the magazine with an intention of putting our school on the map once again. Good news for them and for us all, the article was published and it was on the magazine for whole of the Kenyan High schools to read. The bad news was the article was written to *diss* several rival schools around Meru County. These were schools we had interacted with and likely to interact with occasionally. Some were the girl's school we liked most. For example Materi Girls High School, St. Mary's Girls High School, Kaaga Girls High School. Some were the boy schools that we despised most like Kanyakine Boys

High School. Most of them were the top schools in Meru County; Nkubu Boys High School and Meru Boys High School.

The criticism was taken differently: we made great enemies with a few school and sweethearts with one; Materi Girls High School. This was just about how it all began. But here we are now several months afterwards.

We were in Form 4, almost 2 years after the Insider Magazine incident. We were invited to a Scouts club function in our now sister school, Materi Girls. We loved to visit their school way too much. For most of us who do not know about this beautiful school; it is one of the best that there is. I can say the common high school rules are unheard off. They are allowed to live a civilian kind of life in school. They do shopping like a civilian would do. They had a bakery at school. They ate nice food. And when I talk of nice food, kindly trust I know what nice food is. At least in comparison with what we used to have in our school. They were allowed to have FM tuners in school to listen to Easy FM and Kiss 100. They had few or no afternoon classes.

Those were definitely privileges that you could not find in a normal high school; at least back then. They were an example of how high schools should be structured. Their grades were far much better than any school with the strictest rules like ours.

On top of that, they were the most beautiful lot of teenage girls in the entire Meru County. To some extent I think they were handpicked and then admitted to the school. Even well-known boys school were heads over heels for them. But we had found favor in their hearts; thanks to the unique commonality we had. They were a catholic sponsored school and so were we. We would meet in functions that our competitors would only dream of. We had the upper hand and we took the advantage to win their hearts.

Back to our story; so we attended the scout club event at their school, at the heart of Meru South. Several other schools were invited; within Meru county and neighboring Embu County. The latter was represented by the one and only Nguviu Boys High School. The former was represented by the very able St. Pius X Seminary and our dear rivals Kanyakine Boys. There were several others but somehow we did not notice them. We know the eyes of the frog do not stop a buffalo from quenching its thirst but it can reconsider in case of the eyes of a crocodile. They were the frog eyes and the two; Kanyakine Boys and Nguviu boys were the crocodile eyes.

The function was a total success; my school mates, mostly my classmates were winning more hearts to us by rocking the event. I had just met a lady that up to that moment had the most beautiful eyes I had ever seen. They were the Chinese type but now with all the grace, elegance and curves that a Kenyan woman comes in. She was light skinned and I had this thing for light-skinned, gorgeous eyes, curvy ladies. So your guess is as good as mine; I did not want much to do with what the event was offering. I was home and dry with, let me call her Fiona. I spent the best part of the day downloading the poems that I had crammed the previous weeks prior to the function on her beautiful self.

When it was time for lunch, Fiona saved me the trouble of eating a loaf of bread and a 500ml of Sprite soda and invited me to dine with her. I was at the top of the world and little did I know of the tension mounting at the hall where the function was happening. In the battle of supremacy against our school and Kanyakine Boys, a few people were kicked between the legs. They had vowed to expose the boys and the men. In one way or another battle was on and it was unclear what direction it was ended. The point was to outsmart the rival and get the biggest wild scream from our hosts. The guys break-danced their bones, they rapped their hearts out and tried every way possible to be the best in the activities.

I was surprised when I heard a huge commotion at the hall; the kind that says, "Hell has broken loose". This meant a premature end of my time with Fiona. A friend motioned to me that we need to run for our bus immediately. A fight between our school and Kanyakine Boys had started and it was getting messy. Several other schools were caught in the crossfire. I hurriedly hugged Fiona goodbye and as the gentleman that I was I instructed her to head to the hostel until the skirmishes were over.

Stones were being hurled around. Visiting students were running towards their schools buses that had started to flee the school as a strategy to stop the fight. Thank you to my basketball playing, I was fit enough to run for the bus without a sweat. I also did not stop a flying rock; I was well, unscathed. Then the unthinkable happened; our school bus was not as lucky as I was. It stopped a rock missile launched by Kanyakine Boys with it rear emergency door and it broke. Infuriated with this, some of my school mates stepped up to launch a counter attack. After a few throws, I heard a confirmation that they had successfully brought down the windscreen of Kanyakine Boys Bus. Eye for an eye is the saying but I think in this case it was head for feet. They were to drive back to school without the windscreen and we were to drive without the emergency exit door.

I could only imagine what was waiting for us when we got back to school. I knew our principal; or rather Rector as he was referred to as, would eat us for dessert that evening. The patron of the scouts club was dumbfounded. He could not believe how things had turned south so quickly. The scouts club was the most disciplined club in the whole school. But the battle of supremacy in mars usually throws the honor code out of the window. He knew he had a report to give and a reputation to protect or worse to rebuild.

It was too late to turn things around; this was the new reality and we all had to deal with it as a team. We resorted to face the consequences together. Even those that were busy with Fiona, read me, and did not know what the heck happened were to accept the repercussions. I have always been a team player and I had no issue with that, but it meant a possible suspension. To be precise, a possible first suspension since I joined school more than ten years ago. My parents would skin me or even worse chew on me out of anger.

It was on a Saturday. We got to school, all evening nothing was said from the administration about the events of the day. On Sunday, we were waiting for our judgment but still nothing happened. We began to ease up concluding that the administration thought that we did what we had to do. We went to the extent of making fun of the events of the previous day's event. We started recreating the scenes and giving detailed word video to those who did not see it frame by frame.

Then Monday happened. It was a custom to go for a morning church service every day in our school. The priest leading on that day was none other than the Boss of the School, The Principal and The Rector. All was going well; he did not show any signs of being mad about anything. We had developed ways and means to read the climatic conditions of our admin. Or so we thought; maybe he was filled with the Holy Spirit during the church service that left him no sooner than he concluded the service.

He began like he was telling a story of some goons; oh sorry you used the battalion, who went to throw dirt at the name of our well decorated school. He narrated all exaggerated events of what happened two days earlier. Someone had fed him some rotten Intel but we stood no chance to recuse them. He said that this was a crime that could not go unpunished. He ordered all the 62 of us to meet him at the administration block after breakfast.

We thought he would call a few well respected teachers in the area of administering corporal punishment and then start a "correction ritual". We had no idea what was waiting for us. To our surprise, he handed each of us an envelope whose contents were only supposed to be opened after getting out of the schools gate. We were being suspended. He gave us 15 minutes to prepare to leave and so we did.

My class, Form 4A had the most culprits. Most of us school captains and prefects. This is the moment I came to realize sometimes leadership equals being radical. We were to go home for a week and then come back with Ksh. 2000 for cover for the damages and bring our parents. This was definitely going to be a tough one for me. But I had a bargaining chip; I was not the only one suspended. It was a group suspension and I just happened to be in the wrong place at the wrong time. My dad would understand this for sure, I consoled myself.

Now remember I said my high school is 6 kilometers from my village. So I got home before most people could figure out a way to get home. I found my family having breakfast and I joined them. Nobody asked why I was home and I was not in a hurry to cough it out. After breakfast I handed my dad the letter and as I expected a 30 minutes lecture followed. Several episodes of this were to be witnessed in the following one week until I got back to school. I would be reminded over a dozen times why I was taken to school. I was taken to school to study and pass well not go to functions in girl schools or worse pick fights with other schools.

Anyway this passed nice and easy and we were on to the next big thing. We were in form 4 but this did not stop us from living it up in school. That was one in a series of 2 other suspensions that I got in my forth form.

Fortunate for me, they were group suspensions. I was just a guy taking the bullets for the team.

The second one came when one of our classmates got sick and succumbed to his illness. We blamed this on the administrations negligence of student welfare and lack of proper hygiene. There was some type of stomach related outbreak in school and we had to do something about it. We raised several other issues that contributed to the demise of our brother and we wrote a letter to the Boss. A decision was anonymously reached that we would peacefully strike only to come back to school a week later on condition that the school will implement our suggestions to stop any unnecessary deaths. The next day we peacefully walked out of the schools gate and went home leaving the rest of the school with mouths wide open. The form 4s had abandoned the school and we were committed to making sure no other single life is lost.

To cut the long story short, we got back after one week. I had gone for testing and I was found to be having typhoid and so was the case for a number of other students. At least we had a concrete case. When we got back we found suspension letters waiting for us. There comes suspension number two. We were to go home for a week and bring our parents on the reporting day. I remember this day well since my mother caned me at the instruction of the disciplinary team at school for the first time since when I was maybe 10 years old. And that was 7 years later.

The drama around this was ridiculous but in the end of it, improvements were made and no one got sick due to unhygienic environment.

"The supreme art of war is to subdue the enemy without fighting." – Sun Tzu

---

My third suspension came during my last 3 months in high school when we Form 4s were accused of vandalizing form 1s property during the holiday tuition sessions. Again this was a group suspension, but now it was no longer about being in the wrong group at the wrong time.

I had kept a clean disciplinary track record for 3 years only to break it on my final year. The time I should have been more serious with my school work. When we did our final exam it was a relief to us, the school administration and to our parents too. We were a troublesome class. One thing I know is the events of this final year in high school impacted our lives greatly. It made most of us and I think we are better now than we could ever be if we had different circumstances. We made stupid mistakes, that is for sure, but we took risks too; that is invaluable.

I cannot finish my high school story without mentioning the most stupid thing I ever did. During one of those famous school club functions, I met a beautiful young lady who swept me off my feet because of her long silky hair. This was before I met Fiona of Materi Girls. This lady, let me call her Portia, from Gikumene Girls was anything a grown up man; I thought I was then, would have needed for a wife. She was shy but yet confident enough to say what she wants, she was beautiful and yet did not try to prove it. She was kind and yet ignoble to assure that you can only be hers. The future looked bright from her smile to all her femininity gorgeousness. Looking back to Portia and Fiona, Portia was the must have and Fiona the nice to have. Talking of a meal, Portia was like the main course and Fiona the dessert. Anyone one sane enough would take the main meal.

Therefore Portia was my high school flame. Being a loyal man I had vowed to get involved with no one else because I had found my ride or die. So it came to this time when I was in form 4. It was a few weeks before starting my final exam. Portia had not replied to my last three letters. I was worried because the window was closing on me to ever see her again. We did not have the luxury of abundant cellular devices like we do now. The best way to communicate was only via letters, notes or word of mouth through friends. Desperate times call for desperate measures. It happened that there was an event at their school that we were not officially invited. Some of my classmates; the dancers saw it as an insult and decided to find means to crash the party nonetheless. On my side I saw an opportunity to reconnect with my love or at least get a closure on why she went MIA on me. The plan was to use the schools backdoor, (read breaking out through the fence) and then head to Gikumene Girls that was just 8-9 Kilometers away from our school. I bought the plan, and for the first time in my life as a student, I broke the biggest of the school rules. I was suspended 3 times in a group but this would have been my first personal suspension had I been caught.

It would have been all for what? For a fantasy lady that wanted nothing to do with me and actually she was not the most beautiful. I was so blinded by teenage hormonal imbalance that I threw my character out of the window. But I got a lesson from it; a lesson that when I love, I love for real. I am all in and I would do anything to keep my word. Just saying, maybe someone needed to hear this for the sake of the future.

"When we meet someone and fall in love, we have a sense that the whole universe is on our side. And yet if something goes wrong, there is nothing left! How is it possible for beauty that was there only minutes before to vanish so quickly? Life moves very fast. It rushes from heaven to hell in a matter of seconds." – Paulo Coelho

---

CHAPTER 3

WELCOME TO REAL LIFE

November 11th 2009 the final day of my high school life. It was the day we sat for the last examination paper. Everyone was excited and hopeful for the life ahead. It was a new beginning; which comes with uncertainty and anxiety in equal measure. Despite of the latter we all were glad that this life was over and now we were on transition to something much better. Nobody cared much about what to do after that moment, all we wanted was go home and enjoy the sense of freedom that the graduation from high school came with. The worst mistake you could do was to ask me what I wanted to be at that point in time.

Home we went, the freedom we enjoyed. Sleeping till late into the day, listening to music all day long with no one reminding you to study, it was refreshing. Days were moving quickly; 2009 turned into 2010 which I was looking forward to eagerly. I was to get an opportunity to attend a wedding. It was the first one in my family since I was only but a child. My uncle was getting married and not from my village but from a few counties away. I was excited in two ways: one I was to get an opportunity to travel and second, I was to get a new Aunt. I have always had a special place for Aunt in my heart.

I do not remember much about the wedding but I remember how awesome it was mingling with people of another tribe in such an intimate occasion. I remember noticing the excitement of getting to explore and learn more about other cultures. I remember getting the feel of marrying outside your tribe being such an interesting thing. I know I still had my eyes on my Amerucan beauty Portia but I remember wishing that she was from another background. A new perspective was opened in my mind's eye and all over sudden I became a multi culture enthusiast. The wedding was a success to the new couple and to me for the revelation I got. This was the beginning of a real interest in different culture and the interest to marry from another culture was ignited (story for another time).

Another thing that really excited me was the fact that I could use my community library membership to read exciting novels. I have always liked reading especially when I know there will be no tests at the end. My hunger for reading well told stories was awakened by my high school teacher Mr. Kabonyi. The name was given to him after one of the characters in one of our literature set books The River Between by Ngugi wa

Thiong'o. He was quite an interesting teacher; a great entertainer and a performer to the core. He was the real definition of a literature teacher.

When we were reading the play "Shreds of Tenderness" by John Luganda I totally loved literature and storytelling; thanks to my able teacher. The book illustrates how people take advantage of political instability to enrich self or engage in activities that benefit their greed for property or sexual desires and other immoralities. I loved the way the characters were represented, the words they used and how Mr. Kabonyi brought them to life. He used to play the role of Odie; a main character in the play, during the class reading. My favorite phrase still rings in my head to date:

Odie: I could have puked when I saw you hugging and toasting each other like bamboozled baboons in a dionysiac trance.

Mr. Kabonyi by help of Shreds of tenderness and another play titled "An Enemy of the People" by Henrick Isben got me interested in literature. That is about the same time I started collecting quotes from the famous people of the past centuries and started writing some poems. From then to date I am so in love with any literary work, from books to movies to music.

With that said and done you can now imagine how many novels I devoured after gaining the freedom from the school system. I read some Danielle Steel, some Sidney Sheldon and so many of other novelists I cannot remember the names. I majored in love stories and romantic novels. I developed a strong vocabulary and romantic quotes that I used to terrorize sisters on Facebook. I would easily sweep them off their feet with just a few comments about anything.

You might be wondering; how now? How can you be swept off your feet by just a statement about your voice? Well, picture this; you are an 18 year old, very young and restless. Then someone as handsome as this brother writing these words says to you, "The rippling sound of your voice is like a lilting breeze over my heart. Your soothing touch heals me and makes me soar. We whisper and our breaths mingle. We caress and our souls kiss. We make love and we love. We are two coming together to be one. And so we are defined and defining".

Big words right? That is courtesy of a book I read. I still have the phrase in my head. Could I have had the same memory for mathematical formulas and procedures may be life would have been super different, HAHA! Anyway I would not wish to have it otherwise.

My passion for books and literature has definitely evolved but I cannot forget where it all started. This single passion has shaped my life in ways you cannot imagine as you will find out later. For now I can mention that through reading I was able to improve my English and tone down on my not-so-desired Amerucan accent.

"Desire without knowledge is not good – how much more will hasty feet miss the way!" Proverbs 19:2 [NIV]

The year 2010 came to me at the full force that a year can afford. I realized that am no longer a high school kid that could rely on his parents for pocket money. I realized I had to get my hands dirty and start earning some money for myself. There were 2 options. One labor for my parents with hope of getting monetary rewards; this would be impractical because my parents are not the type to pay their children to do what they are expected to do. Two, to practice farming. In my village especially at that time there were not many options for a high school graduate.

My best bargain was to apply the Agriculture I learnt in school in the farm. My dad was really excited about it when I asked him for a portion of *shamba* to plant my own tomatoes with his support. He had a plan to do the same crop as it was around February and the season to plant tomatoes in my village. We would run the projects side by side. What could go wrong with the mentorship of my over qualified dad? I reasoned. I was confident that in a few weeks it would be a bumper harvest.

My plan was to make some money and upgrade my phone which was a second hand Motorola L7i that I bought from my cousin. (Writing this down I just remembered that I never paid fully for it. I need to call my cousin to apologize HAHA.) I wanted something more decent like Motorola W5, which was a flap phone. That was something fancy; it supported GPRS to log in to Facebook and MySpace and could download the 2go app. We did not know the Smartphone was about to wipe them all out.

Farming is quite an interesting activity and occupation. I thought I had it all figured out from my class work. I realized there was some really tough work to be done.

First, I had to wake up at 6am to water my plants lest they be scorched to death under the ruthless February sun. They I would repeat the same in the evening. This was to continue until the seedlings were completely established; when they have developed new roots and have brand new leaves.

Second, I had to handle the headache of caterpillars that were harvesting my tomato seedling by eating the stems for lunch. You can imagine looking for caterpillars in the soil to terminate them so that they do not eat the replacement.

Third, tomatoes require strict attention: weeding was a headache. God bless my mum she helped me get the job done. My dad was there to guide not to do it for me. Fourth, propping the tomatoes after they had started flowering and bearing fruits was a tough one, from sourcing the proper propping sticks, to supporting the tomatoes using threads from dry banana plant barks.

It was challenging as much as it was interesting and educative. Farmers ought to be some of the most patient people on earth. In addition they ought to be the best examples to give when talking of the law of process. At this point I realized why Jesus Christ used farmers in His parables to teach.

---

*"Farmers who wait for the perfect weather never plant.
If they watch every cloud, they never harvest."
Ecclesiastes 11:4 [NLT]*

I knew I was learning a priceless life lesson and besides that I was to earn my very first income. The first income from my sweat, my hand work and my efforts was in the offing. Of course my dad was a great contributor because he gave me all the farm inputs; fertilizer and agrichemicals.

Then the unthinkable happened. Just at that point when the tomatoes have sizeable fruits, just a few more days to start harvesting, they were attacked by tomato disease called blight. To those who do not know what blight is; it is to tomatoes what cancer is to human beings. My dad diligently used the necessary fungicides to fight the disease but it got worse. The leaves started blackening and the fruits falling off in just a matter of a week. I told you this is a cousin of cancer only in Kingdom Plantae.

We were wiped out. All the days of hard work were left with nothing to show but nasty looking dying tomato plants. If you thought your work is hard, maybe you should try farming. Things can go south even to the experts. Were it not for the fact that my dad was also a victim of the blight, I would have concluded that my skills were not up to par. But that was not the case, we did our best but our best was not enough. I learnt the art of accepting uncertainty and living with it as a part of life. I realized that you can never really have it all figured out. The experts can be wrong; the knowledgeable can make a fool of themselves and that is life.

That lesson was well learnt; on to the next adventure of life after high school. About the same time that we were being wiped out of our tomato farming dreams the French beans planting time had arrived. The market projections for the French beans were promising. I had recognized yet another opportunity to try my hand in farming. My grandmother was excited about the possibilities in the French beans market. We were almost a month late, 2 weeks late but we were committed to make a cut out of the French beans. My sweet and loving grandma offered me partnership in the French beans project and I took it. She was to provide the piece of land, planting seeds and fertilizer. I was to offer the labor for land preparation, planting and watering, to start with.

This was less troublesome than the tomato farming and was quite a success. Just 2 weeks before we could start harvesting the market had hit a record price of Ksh. 100 per Kilogram of French beans. This was exciting news and we could not wait to get our crop to market.

Two weeks later our first harvest came; it is not usually a big one because most of the beans are not yet market ready. The prices had gone down a little bit but it was still good money. We made approximately Ksh. 1,500 on that first day. Possibilities were to quadruple that amount on the second harvest, double the second on the third and fourth.

The first harvest was able to cover most of the cost of the planting seeds and inputs. Yaaay! We were breaking even already! The second harvest was to set us on a profit making path after covering the expenses completely.

Then the unexpected happened; the prices of the French beans plummeted from the Ksh. 70 that we sold at on the first day to a mere Ksh. 30. This was the most painful part of all these farming. The failure was caused by a natural thing and it was quite understandable. What about this French beans thing? In the bottom of my heart I knew it was a market being controlled by some cartels that did not care much about the farmers who put their sweat and blood into delivering a world class crop like the one we had. Our French beans were so nice that at some point we opted to feed them to the cows and the drink the milk instead of selling it at that throw away price that had further gone down to around Ksh. 20.

At the end of it all after expenses we had only made Ksh. 1500. We split it and I got my Ksh. 800. Remember my goal was buy me a new phone, but at that point that dream was as far as it was when I had not made the decision to practice farming. All I did was change the case of my phone to make it look new. So I spent half of my pay to make up my phone. I got two things from this French bean farming experience; one a scar on my chest below my left shoulder. It happened during the first harvest when I tripped carrying a crate full of French beans. I had a choice to drop it but it was just too precious and therefore my chest paid the price. Second I learnt a lesson for a second time that life is full of surprises and things we cannot anticipate or control.

> *"The secret of success is learning how to use pain and pleasure instead of having pain and pleasure instead of having pain and pleasure use you. If you do that, you're in control of your life. If you don't, life controls you."*
> Anthony Robbins

While all these farming escapades were happening, the KCSE results were released. My biggest fear was not getting a bad grade in all subjects; my greatest fear was that I would fail in Mathematics. I never made this clear enough; in high school Mathematics and I were like water and paraffin. I could make it to the top 10 positions in the class but with a D+ in Mathematics. The best grade I ever got in Mathematics was a C and at that time I was top 3 of the class. That meant everything else I had scored at least a B+ and definitely several A's. That is how bad I was in it. Maybe I could have made it to the first position if I could by any chance make it to a B.

The service to receive the results via text message had just been introduced; it was easy to check the results. Of course everyone was eager to know what I had scored. When they came I was not the first one to know, somehow, regardless of being the one who sent the results request first, mine took time to get a response. My uncle's request was more than prompt. I remember his words so well, "You have passed but Mathematics and Physics have let you down", he said.

I remember the sick feeling in my gut. My thoughts were running into a million directions. I even imagined how my dad would command me to repeat fourth form and try to score a better grade. Oh boy! I was not ready for that. I took his phone and saw the results for myself. I had scored a bold B- overall grade. Every subject with an exception of Mathematics and Physics, I had scored above C+. Mathematics D+ (which we used to refer to as Daudi Msalabani Swahili for 'David on a cross') and physics a C-. The latter did not affect my overall grade as I had done the 3 sciences, Physics, Chemistry and Biology. The Kenya National Examination Council with all their generosity only record the two best scored sciences on your final grade. For me it was Biology and Chemistry which I scored a B+ and a C+ respectively.

What followed was the question I was afraid that would be asked sooner than later. My dad asked, are you okay with that grade or would you like to go back to school? Of course the answer was I am okay with it. I was going to avoid another month in high school at all costs. A board of experts, (read my uncles and aunts) on matters regarding education was set and advice started coming. Some thought it was a great idea I got back to school. Some said that I should take a bridging course for Mathematics. And my favorite is the one who said, why not focus on the subjects he has done pretty well and advise him the career that would suit him?

At the end of the discussion I knew and was also convinced that I would, make it in the medical world since I had a good grade in English, Biology and Chemistry. I wanted to become a Clinical Officer as my grades dictated. But up to date I have a phobia for hospitals. It is not an environment I enjoy being in; no wonder I rarely or rather never get sick. So I had a choice to make, to learn to love the environment and spend the rest of my life there or to find a way out.

Thanks to God, I had just discovered Google. At this point Google would become my friend; a friend that I have kept up to date. I started searching for courses that would suit me. Back then I knew of a few professions: teachers, doctors, accountants, nurses and priesthood. These were what I was introduced to as highly marketable. They were the easiest to get a job in, in other words. Unfortunately for me I wanted nothing to do with any of the above. I wanted something technical, something that has a few rules on how it is done. Something I can have the freedom to invent and dare to be different.

After long nights of trying to understand the professional world, I got more confused than before. I had found out some interesting careers like micro-biology & biotechnology, cardiovascular technologist, nuclear engineering, industrial chemistry and the likes. I was just looking for something that my grades pointed to. Something biological or chemical related. I even took a personality test to see what course would suit me best; I did not know better. My personality test came out as investigative, realistic and enterprising. That matched me up with careers like agricultural & food scientist, biochemist, microbiologist, and psychologist to mention but a few.

When I presented the list to my able consultants, read relatives and friends, they posed questions like, where will you get employed after doing this or that?, how marketable is the course?, and whom do you know that has done the same course?, which college in Kenya is offering that course? They were all great questions, logical and important but I had no answers to them. So I let them talk me out of thinking about them.

Then an idea to apply for the KMTC for a Clinical Officer course started to make more sense. There is ever increasing need for medics and even though I did not like the idea of working in a hospital, I was assured of a lifelong paying career. That is what mattered and I was made to believe it. I was made to believe that my convenience and a well-paying, respectable career moved on parallel paths. I was made to believe that a dream career that you did the things you love to do is non-existent and I had to compromise my desires to conform to the patterns of the society. I was made to believe that I needed to pursue what has been tested and has worked for other people and not wander in unchartered waters. Even if it meant discovering something great at the end of it all, I was forbidden not to take the risk.

The September 2010 KMTC intake was advertised and I made the application for clinical medicine course. My path was set by the societal default setting; pursuing the known. I did not like it but I was promised a good life afterwards; a handsome salary and a decent lifestyle. That was good enough to make me settle back then. I had wrapped my mind around it and the plan was a go for me.

And then God came through to save me from myself and my society norm. The application letter to KMTC through some unexplainable circumstances was not delivered in time. It reached 3 days after application deadline. I was sixty percent relieved, twenty percent disappointed and twenty percent mixed feelings. I was only disappointed because I would stay at home longer; I could not wait to join college.

"The tragedy of life is what dies inside a man while he lives." – Albert Einstein

---

An angel was sent in the form of my favorite Aunt Reg; the only sister my dad has. It happened quite casually as we were just chatting about the possibilities of my career path. Then she mentioned a course that sounded like music to my ears.

She could not articulate it quite well but my friend Google could answer all the questions I had. She even gave me social proof when she said that one of my distant cousins and aunt were indeed pursuing the course. I was swept off of my feet by Telecommunication Engineering and I was all in for this one.

For the first time I had clarity of what I needed to pursue and something that was fulfilling enough. I have always loved technology especially in the information technology sector. It was something that amazed and intrigued me in equal measure. But I was sold on the idea that my passion and what pays lived in a different neighborhood.

There was one problem though, my grades did not say much about my ability to successfully pursue an engineering course. I did not even meet the requirements of the course in any college. My college of choice was Railway Training Institute where my two relatives studied.

My Mathematics and Physics grade were determined to deny me my dream. But I was also determined to show the world that rules are there to bring order and govern not necessarily to be kept. I knew very well that I could not make my application online or via letter. I knew they would throw it away and cut me off. So I resorted to going in there and making a case for myself in the company of Aunt Reg.

I remember the dean of students looking at my grades and giving a fatherly advice. He said that my core subjects did not allow me to take an engineering course and he strongly advised me to consider a business course.

The conversation took around 9 minutes but I stood my ground and said that I want telecommunication engineering or nothing. He saw my determination and resolved to give me an admission on the condition that I would change my course if the going gets tough in the engineering class. I knew that was not going to happen but I quickly agreed.

Coming to Nairobi on that day to make the application was my second time in my life to be in the city. The first was a few years earlier when we came to the Animal Orphanage and Bomas of Kenya on a school trip.

It was one of my most interesting and exciting moments in years. I could not wait to join college and become a full resident of the city. In our village there is this kind of expectation to succeed if you make it to living in the city. Coming to Nairobi was like a sure way to a better life and everyone expects nothing less from you.

From both my parents side only one person was in Nairobi and was the first and only person to ever live in Nairobi. That is in our family; I was about to become the second one. Good for me I had a relative in Nairobi and I was better than someone who had no one to show them around. Well, let us see how my Nairobi residency worked out for me.

CHAPTER 4

POWER TO READ

September 2010 came fast as I wanted it to. I had made a decision to do the seemingly undoable. I was determined to make possible the seemingly impossible. I was on my way to conquer the seemingly unconquerable. I had already set my mind to making Mathematics and all its cousins a testimony.

I was going to prove the system wrong and show it I can do Mathematics. I was going to beat any doubt that existed around me by simply doing what was thought to be impractical and foolish.

As in, who fails in Mathematics and then burdens themselves with an engineering course?

My answer would be, the radical ones; those that choose not to be defined by the system but define themselves through the conscious efforts of working on self.

Aunt Reg was again to help me navigate through the busy Nairobi streets that I was yet to be accustomed to.

She was better placed to take me to college; who else would? Could my mum or my dad take me? They both had no clue of Nairobi City.

My Aunt was a wise one; quite a great navigator. She showed me the easiest path from the Meru bus stop stage aka Tea Room to the main Bus Station where I could board Matatu number 11 bound for South B where I would spend my next 4 years.

She also introduced me to Afya Centre; the building I could use as my compass to find my way to the bus station without having to ask. Back then there was a belief that most 'Nairobians' (people residing in Nairobi) would mislead you if you asked for directions. Learning self-sufficiency matters navigating around the city was of utmost importance.

This was a rebirth, a new beginning, a fresh start to live up to the best of my capacity and become more. I was set on a cause to bring glory to my family; as the first person to go college in my grandpas third generation and the first engineer in the family.

It was so unfortunate that Mr. Rukaria; my grandpa would not be around on my graduation day. He had passed on two years earlier after a short illness. He was a champion of getting education and the decision I made would have made him really proud of me.

My life in Railway Training Institute started on a high note. We were living in the school hostels and I had 3 roommates. Mark was there to pursue mechanical engineering, Harry and Ken Electrical Engineering. It was a room full of engineering hopefuls representing 3 counties. These became defaults friends, those that were brought to me.

Then came my first day in class; I never knew it was to be an old train coach. That was to be our class for the next few months. Looking for a place to do your classes in a stationary train coach? Go to Railway Training Institute. It is the coolest class environment ever. I loved it but I was also underwhelmed because I was expecting that engineering classes took place in workshops full of machines and tools because engineering is practical, or so I thought.

Then I met one of my best friends till to date. Elias was quite a silent man, composed and very good in Mathematics. We became friends on the first day in class and as they say the rest is history. Up to date we are great friends and we have been through a lot together. He became my brother in class and outside, my friend in everything, my coach in Mathematics and other academic stuff, my desk-mate in class, to mention but a few.

Then I met the best mathematics lecturer ever, Mr. Marty. He was the Head of Department of

Telecommunication Engineering and as far as I can tell the best lecturer in the world. He helped me change my attitude towards Mathematics and made learning fun. He always had stories to tell; his class was not just about Calculus and Indices.

He had what I call the human factor that made the inhuman sound fun. I remember him telling us why Mathematics should be a fun thing and not something to worry about. He went to an extent of telling us the best way to revise Mathematics or do assignment was to tune in to your favorite music and as the speakers' blast the melodies you get busy blasting solutions out of Mathematics problems. I took this literary and it worked for me.

Some of my classmates thought of it as a super unconventional method but not me; it was all I needed. I needed something radical to help me associate Mathematics to being easy. Back then I used to love my soul music, so I would tune in to Classic 105 and the Mathematics Mood would tune in automatically. Through this single radical and effective method I was able to get my grades from below pass mark to the zones of an A.

God bless you Lecturer Marty. You changed my view and helped me learn a very vital lesson in life. A lesson that whatever I think I can do or cannot do is just a matter of belief and mindset. With the right thinking I can alter that and change my circumstances.

From cannot to can and vice versa. You taught me that I have the power to design my world in my own terms and throw the rule book out of the window. Ordinary people think that quiet spaces are good for study but you taught me to be abnormal and have fun while I study.

You helped me affirm one of my all-time best quotes by *Arnold J. Toynbee "The supreme accomplishment is to blur the line between work and play."* I was a victim of Mathematics problem but you helped to create a hero out of it.

"Do not conform to the pattern of this world but be transformed by the renewing of your mind..."
Romans 12:2 [NIV]

I had cracked the code of passing in Mathematics and I was so proud of myself. I realized I was never bad at it. I was never taught properly. I had proved Mathematics wrong and nothing was going to stop me from pursuing my course. The offer by the dean of students to change course was now officially off my table. If he is a patient man he is probably still waiting for me to go tell him that he was right to say I could not handle an engineering course, 9 years later.

At this point in time if I was to get any challenge in my studies, you can be sure that it was not Mathematics related. Actually there were tougher things than Mathematics. Up to date I have never really internalized Kirchhoff's Theorem and Norton's Theorem. And trust me I have no intentions to getting back to it at all cost.

I had one problem though, we were being trained to work in the 21st century world but we used all old technology. To make it worse 99.9% of it was theory. We studied a Microprocessor chip called 8085; something that was used at the dawn of information technology.

Up to date I fail to understand how the school system syllabuses are developed and as a result I have a huge grudge with the school system. It does not get us ready for the real world; it has become like a cultural rite of passage with no big impact in the lives of those that go through it.

Something really needs to change. We need more radical visionaries like my Lecturer Marty in leadership positions to evolve this animal that has remained the same for centuries.

Enough with the rant, I just had to get it off my chest. It was really tough studying practical things in theory. And even more tough studying obsolete technology knowing that there was no practical use for it in the real world. As we will talk about in this book, *"The Amerucan Dream"* is a baby born out of the need to bring change to the way we view education. Let us talk about that later.

Now that Mathematics was out of my way, my college life was set to be blissful. One of my ambitions from Primary School was to get an opportunity to play basketball at a competitive level. I learnt a few things about the game when I was in high school but unfortunately our school was not participating in school games out of some disciplinary issues of our predecessors.

I never got appropriate coaching on the game. I was determined to make my college basketball career more productive and I was all in. From the first week in college, the basketball court was my favorite most spot. Every day at 4:15pm you would find me on the basketball court no matter the weather, no matter the day of the week.

On the basketball court I was working hard to make up for what I lacked in skills and exposure with effort and repetition. I was told that repetition is the mother of mastery. The more I shot the basketball the more I became accustomed to it and what did not feel natural started to become second nature.

Basketball became my drug; I could not get enough of it. I would rush to the basketball any time of the day when I was free and I have a basketball with me. It is the only game I will never need an opponent for me to enjoy. Basketball by itself is just enough company for anyone to draw pleasure out of it by themselves. Darkness was the villain in my basketball stories; it is the only thing that got me off the court.

Looking back, basketball actually saved my life and my education. Here is why. We all know how physical activity is important for anyone who wishes to perform on an optimum level. Basketball did that for me. Also while my friends were scheming on how to fornicate, I was busy shooting one more basket and sharpening my basketball handling skills. While my friends were idle, drinking alcohol and watching soccer on weekends, I was busy sweating on the court, working on my cardio or perfecting my lay-up.

So when I say basketball saved my life it really did. I lost many girlfriends because I could not make enough time to be with them. They complained all I did was go to class and play basketball. And yes they were right; those were my biggest activities in college.

In 2011 the KETISA (Kenya Technical Institutes Sports Association) Ball games were to be held at the end of July by then Eldoret Polytechnic. Of course I was all in to make sure that I got selected as part of the team representing our institution.

From around February 2011 we were already in preparation for the games 5 months away. We knew we were meeting the very best from around the country and we were not going to leave our participation to chance. We were determined to not only represent but also win a trophy for the Institute.

Play after play, drill after drill, dribble after a dribble, shot after shot, we worked on all aspects of a successful basketball match. We trained for endurance and strength, those that needed to lose some weight did and those who needed to gain some mass did. We had no professional coach in any of it all, but as the old saying says; make up for what you lack in providence by hard work, we did so.

The trip to Eldoret was my first since joining college and also the first time to go to Eldoret, the home of champions. It was both exciting and insightful; I had this urge to get out and see how other cultures live and this was a fulfillment of that need.

Eldoret is usually cold around July just like most places in Kenya around that time. Before this visit I thought my village was the coldest place. In 'Eldy', as it is commonly known, it can be cold to the point of water from the pipes turned white, almost solidifying to ice.

A tough experience it was; we were expected to shower with that same water and your guess is as good as mine, many of us skipped the shower. It was better to be rained on than to step into the shower with cold Eldoret water.

Let us talk about the most exciting part of the visit, the game days. Just like any other basketball tournaments we started in group stages. The first two teams were to advance to the next round. I cannot quite remember the teams in our groups but I definitely remember that the hosts, Eldoret Polytechnic got the first position and we were second.

We easily proceeded to the quarter final stage and we won 3 games out of 4. We got ourselves a chance at the semis and the dream to win the trophy was closing in on us. But in the semis, things are not as easy as the earlier stages of the tourney. The teams play harder, they are more focused on getting a slot at the Finals and it was a win or go home situation. Nobody wanted to go home, so let us fight for the two slots at the finals.

We were facing the best of the best; the hosts Eldoret Polytechnic were there, Technical Development Institute, The fierce Kisumu Polytechnic was there too. Every game was a neck to neck; nobody really took a huge lead for a longtime.

For those who understand the game of basketball you know that anytime your opponent scores you also have a chance to score. This was the affair; you score I score, you turnover I also turnover or better transition to beat you at your own mistake. Up to date this was one of the best basketball games I have ever played.

At the end of it, we found ourselves advancing to the finals. Looking back I know it was not by might or by power but by the grace of God. We had all odds stacked against us. Not only were we underdogs but also we had some of the shortest players in the tournament. I am 511 but I felt like a dwarf on that court. We had people who were 610 and many who were above 6ft. In basketball an extra inch is always advantageous, but we made up for what we lacked in height with wit.

We were facing the fierce Kisumu Polytechnic at the finals. I call them fierce since they were tall and were well seasoned basketball players. Rumors had it that most of them play for the Nyanza Side Kenya Basketball League, Lakeside Club.

This was to be toughest game of them all. It was the finals and nobody was leaving anything to chance. We were not to get any chance to re-do this. From the officials of the game to us and to our opponents, we all observed everything keenly.

Time outs were called as frequently as the game rules allowed. Time was taken to calculate every defensive play and more time used to discuss successful offensive plays. Every successful defense and every single basket brought us one step towards winning the trophy.

The cheering squad was a main part of the game, giving moral support to their team while demoralizing the opponents in subtle ways.

By the 3rd quarter, it was hard to say who would win. The game was getting intense and emotional. Then I realized that if you are playing with someone who out-weighs you in every aspect of the game, the best way to beat them is to throw them off their game. Playing a mind game with them and make them impatient.

Because of their ego, they will end up making mistakes that you can convert into your benefit. This is what we did with the fierce people from the lakeside. Soon they were all out of their game as they were all fouling and sending us to the free-throw line. We took advantage of this especially in the 4th quarter. We went neck to neck and by the final whistle, the scores were a tie.

"Just Play. Have fun. Enjoy the Game." –
Michael Jordan

A basketball game takes around 48minutes comprising of 4 quarters of 12 minutes each but I think for this one we spent not less than 2 hours. It was that thorough. On extra time, the game was even tougher. At this moment, I knew that time was the only determinant of who will win. Whoever who was ahead in scores when time was over was to be the winner. The point was just to be ahead of the opponent.

I could not believe it when the final whistle was blown and one of our men sent to the free throw line after a last second foul. We were behind the opponent by 1 point. If he scored the 2 possible points we would win. The game was already over. The whole court had eyes on this guy. A huge silence followed just when he stepped on the free throw zone. You could hear everyone hold their breaths.

There comes a moment of truth.

He took a deep breath and did all the basics of releasing tension from his body to take a perfect shot. Swish! The first shot was converted, the scores are now tied and we took some time to celebrate that. He went back to the free throw zone, deep breath, relaxed his shoulders, went down on an athletic stance with feet shoulder width apart, and sprung up to send the ball to the basket.

Swish!

Basket good, the referee exclaimed and we were officially the champions of KETISA Basketball 2011. I had the most fulfilling celebration to date; this was a dream come true. Playing basketball in a competitive environment and belonging to the winning team.

We were too busy on the court to notice the Sports Journalist from Nation Media Group. We only realized their presence when we were travelling back to Nairobi when someone called to say that they saw us on the Daily Nation Newspaper.

This was a beautiful experience. I learnt that with a great team working in synergy and God as the centerpiece you can conquer the seemingly unconquerable. Beating Kisumu Polytechnic was unimaginable, it was thought impossible. Even to them they knew they would beat us in a nice and easy way. But all they saw in us was the tip of an iceberg. We had a huge thing going on beneath us, we were stronger than they saw and that is why we beat them.

2011 was the best basketball year in college. I continued playing but we never won any other tournament but we definitely had fun playing for the love of the game. I later joined a basketball club sponsored by a local church around the school and we continued doing the best we could on the court under the Nairobi Basketball Association Division 2 League.

> *"Champions aren't made in gyms. Champions are made from something they have deep inside them – a desire, a vision. They have to have the skill, and the will. But the will must be stronger than the skill."*
> *– Muhammad Ali*

My college life was not all about basketball and engineering. Though they took the main portion of everything, they were not the only thing. After my first year, I was given an opportunity to go for an industrial attachment. It was supposed to run from September to December 2011. By God's grace I was able to secure an attachment with one of the leading Telecommunications services firm in Nairobi.

If you use Zuku internet and cable TV service that was installed around 2011 chances are I am the one who did the work. It was fun learning new things that we could only dream of in the engineering class. As I already highlighted, what they taught in class and what was in the real world was like night and day. This attachment was the best telecommunication engineering class I could ever attend.

I learned things that mattered in the world not in the school system. Then I realized the Mathematics that was disturbing me was not really applicable in the field. I only used Mathematics during an interview when one of the panelists asked me to integrate x^2. I got it wrong but I got the attachment, so it is not my now improved Mathematics that was responsible for my successful interview.

I am not trashing education; no I would never do that. I do not know where I would be if it were not for it. I highly respect it, what am trying to bring out is that education by itself is not enough. It is just a piece of the puzzle that makes a better life. As my High school physics teacher used to say, Education is just there to strengthen your brain muscle. It is a means not a destination. It is the tool not the activity.

My industrial attachment was quite fruitful, career wise and socially too. During one of my routine service delivery at Nairobi's Kilimani Area, I met a client who became a great friend. She is quite a kind and hospitable young lady; I could not help but give her the best service I could manage.

All the cables were neatly clipped and the equipment well arranged. We are always obliged to take care of those people who show us the slightest of kindness. I also did not want to leave a mess in a well-kept Nairobi uptown house.

After the service my client, let me call her Gina, was kind enough to serve us a glass of cold juice and tipped us for a job well done. Being on attachment then, we were not on the company's payroll so tip was highly appreciated.

I do not remember much about how I managed to keep in touch with her after that day. But all I know since then up to date she is a great friend. A friend that you keep for more than 7 years is a real friend.

My advice to you is to never look down on your service man; they might be one of your best friends, just saying.

I am proud to announce that Gina is the only lady I know personally who likes basketball as much as I do. She does not play but she knows that Boston Celtics is not a soccer club in the UK and she knows that LeBron James is not a pop-star. What I mean is that we can have a real basketball conversation and resonate.

She understands what a triple double is, what NBA all-star is, she knows the roles of the basketball team positions. I also believe she understands the basketball rules. Last time I checked she was a great fan of King James and I bet she moved with him to LA Lakers in the 2018-2019 season.

I am just reminded that it has been a while since we last talked basketball with her. She will confirm to me if this season she is rallying behind James and Lakers franchise.

By the time my attachment was ending in early December 2011, I had a great experience at work and I had moved around Nairobi quite well. I was well acquainted with the places that matter in the city; thanks to the nature of my job.

On completion, we were awarded recommendation letters that were to help us seek for employment later after completing our studies. As an appreciation, we were also given Ksh. 6,800 for the job well done.

With this cash I was to fulfill my goal of upgrading my phone. I was able to buy my first smart-phone, the famous Huawei Ideos. It was a used phone but the technology it brought with it, was awesome. We started to upgrade from 2go to Nimbuzz and then came WhatsApp. Of course Facebook was the main social media site of the time.

On my second year of school I met another lifelong friend whom we started off as one of my roommates. My Friend Ken is one of the funniest guys you will ever meet.

Our friendship even grew stronger when we moved into a room of two. We shared the taste of music and I had introduced him to studying with music playing.

There is nothing more fulfilling than being congruent to the desires of someone you live with under the same roof and using the same resources like a stereo radio.

Any music he played I liked and any music I played he liked. We were not in the same class but we really cheered each other up.

We were and up to date are brothers. He has always had my back since then and I always have his.

We did funny and stupid things together that I cannot help but mention. In college we did not have much money to celebrate birthdays. And we also cared less of how we celebrated them as long as it was fun.

We would go to the nearby supermarket buy several bags of popcorns and milk. That is then normal part of it. The abnormal part of it, we would go into our hostel room, clean the table, pour the popcorns on the table, pour the milk in cups and then have an eating competition.

The rules were simple, play *Kool & The Gang's Celebrate Good Times song* and get started but remember not to use your hands even when sipping the milk. And that was birthdays for us. Abnormal yes but we had fun, we appreciated a good old laugh and uplifting music and we never disappointed ourselves on that.

We both knew that we would make it in life because we were hard working engineering students who knew how to mix hard work with play. We knew nothing would stop us from passing our final exams.

We burnt the midnight oil studying when circumstances demanded that. Ken had better discipline in study than I did but maybe it was because his course was tougher than mine. He was pursuing Mechanical Engineering.

Or maybe because I liked to play way too much, most evenings after class he would go study and I would not miss basketball for the world. Anyway, we both passed well in final exams and graduated at the top of both our classes.

So did my other friend, brother and classmate Elias.

"Education is our passport to the future, for tomorrow belongs to the people who prepare for it today." – Malcolm X

Did I get into any relationship while in college? You might be wondering. Ever since my teenage heart was broken by Portia my High School flame, I had learnt a lesson to keep off ladies.

Not that I did not get involved but it was hard to open up myself to really love anyone. To me it equaled being heartbroken sooner than later. So I kind of became a heart breaker. Fulfilling the old saying that, hurt people hurt, broken people break.

I never let anything to get serious; if it started getting serious I would go MIA without explanation.

Looking back I can now treat heartbreakers with kindness because most of them are just producing what they have been through. People who have been badly hurt will definitely hurt you. We can only give what we have.

Like my favorite book says that out of the heart of a man, flows the issues of life. We only reproduce what we have fed ourselves and I was doing exactly that.

Back then I did not understand the self-sabotage and denial that I was living in matters relating with the opposite sex. It felt alright, and besides I was able to keep many female friends without anyone snooping around for my actions and zero commitments.

I recognized my pattern when I was in my final year and I promised myself to change for the better. About the same time, I met Beryl, a freshman, gorgeous, curvy (I have always been interested in body sculpturesque, pardon my human nature if that sounds shallow to you) endowed in all her Kikuyu glory.

She had a very fair light skin, almost flawless and delicate as a piece of Meissen china. She was a lady to adore, love and be proud of. Meeting her reminded me how it felt to be in love with someone.

She completely healed the wound left by Portia and I was now myself. I could love and I could commit. I could see our future together.

She did not complain about my excess attention to basketball and I liked it. She supported my efforts at the court, the best gift a man could ever ask for from the woman they love. We spent most of the evenings together just talking. It was one of the most fulfilling moments off the basketball court. All things were going on well until a wave of gossip hit.

Up to date I do not really understand what happened all I know is she had started seeing someone behind my back. That is the punishment you get for having no money to buy potato chips for your college girlfriend. Someone was buying my girlfriend some outside school catering on my behalf. We all know in such a situation you will be playing a losing game if you talk yourself into staying.

Yes I was broke, and I paid heavily for it. This was an insult which is worse to a man than a heart break. My Amerucan ego would not allow me to stay in the relationship so I called it quits. We had only been together for less than four months. Four beautiful months were all washed down the toilet by a plate of chips *'mwitu'*.

At this point in time I was a little more emotionally strong and I easily moved on. I made a decision to always raise my standards anytime a relationship does not work. That is a code I have lived by till this time. It applies even to friendships and even mentors.

Anytime something does not work, I do not want to make the same mistake, if I am to make a mistake let it be a different one.

If someone could not stay with you because you could not buy chips for them, next date someone who does not like chips or can afford their own chips. Simple!

After a few months later, a close friend who knew about the above story started to find favor in my eyes. If there could be anything between us, this could be the real definition of raising standards. Not only was she beautiful she also had a character to match; talk of the woman in Proverbs 31:10 onwards. When we became friends I thought she was too much for me to handle and yes I was right. She was not a lady to condone my nonsense back then.

But now I had a moment of transformation after meeting Beryl. I was a better man, almost graduating from college and soon to have a job. I felt I was ready for the real thing with a real person like Fifi.

The beauty and the grace of the *Taita* in her needed a real man and I was ready to develop myself to step up to such standards. After Beryl I was completely done with short ladies and as I said Fifi was a true definition of raised standards. She was tall, a nice dark skin to match.

I made my intentions known to her and it caught her with great delight and surprise. Somehow she liked me but just like me she had not thought of a possibility of us dating. It was during my last days in college and she had already finished her course earlier. Then she asked me a question I would advise my daughter to ask any man who gets interested with them. She asked, "You are now out of college, what are your plans in life? What do you want to achieve?"

Thank God it was on a text message. If it was face to face she would have seen the shock and the fear on my face. I really did not know what I wanted out of life; the specifics or what I wanted to achieve. And that scared me to death.

The fact that she asked me such a question meant that I was supposed to give her a concrete answer before we could ever become anything. Honestly I did not have the answer to that question. She advised that I should go get the answers and come back to her if it will not be too late. I was wiped out like a mosquito. I felt small for the fact that I did not know what I wanted out of life. I felt useless for not being able to answer such a quality question asked by the woman of my dreams.

I promised her that even though I did not have it all figured out back then, I would get a clear picture of it and one day she will see it for herself without the need of me pointing it to her.

I highlighted that I would be the best in what I decide to do and that she would not miss it. I thanked her for opening my eyes with that quite intimidating question and we both moved separate ways.

We kept in touch, but once in a blue moon. She is those people you just want to keep around you because they mean a lot to you. Less than two years later she was blessed with a bouncing baby boy. I remember it was around my birthday when I visited them back in 2016; it was the first time to meet since college days.

Looking at her life back then and comparing it to mine I realized why we could not become a couple. We were moving at different directions and different speeds. It was the moment I got a full closure and let things be as they had worked out for everyone's good.

Meanwhile, Fifi and I shared a mutual friend called Felly. Why are the names starting with F? You might ask. The answer is it is because they did. I have altered the names to protect the identity of the people but I have maintained small details like the first letter.

So Felly was my number two in line with the new raised standards. We met at the Nairobi Agricultural Show; I was in my second year.

Yes we were in the same college but our paths never crossed until that time. She was with the schools catering department and I was with the engineering department to exhibit our inventions.

It happened that on one of the days we really got hungry and it was supper hours away. Like if she was heaven sent she came and asked me and a few other colleagues if we were hungry. Of course we were. She brought us *chapatis* that she had just finished cooking for the schools restaurant. And from that act we became great friends up to date. I later found out that she and Fifi were best friends. It does not kill to have two beautiful friends who know each other, does it? Time would tell.

Now that things did not work out with Fifi it was time to move on along the food chain. There is nowhere in the law written that you should never try to date best friends back to back Ha-ha!

So that fact did not even hit my radar. Felly was second in command and was now promoted to be the first in command. Felly was one of the most mature and well brought up lady I knew.

She had the kindness of big sister, generosity of a grandma, no nonsense attitude of mother, and warmth of a person you want to be close to. Then top it all up with her *Kalenjin* beauty that surpasses the rest in her tribe.

Her cooking skills were second to none and her joyful nature therapeutic and refreshing. What else would one ask from the woman they want to send in the family way some day?

With her, I did not want to rush things. I wanted to take calculated moves lest I be asked a question in the class of what are your plans in life. I made sure we talked a lot and we met occasionally but frequently. She had also finished her studies ahead of me but we did not get any closer up until I was also out of college. After a few months of long late night chats and meetings over tea I decided to take things to the next level.

If you remember my uncle's wedding just after I completed high school, I said something about marriage and cultural diversion. At the wedding I was taught from within the need to marry from a different culture. From the few love stories I have shared so far you can tell that I was serious about it.

Up to date I still am sold on this and I live multi-cultural. From the look of things, I will definitely marry from a different tribe, by God's grace. No one am interested in is from Ameru decent.

"A wise woman builds her home, but a foolish woman tears it down with her own hands" Proverbs 14:1 [NLT]

CHAPTER 5

EARNING A LIVING

My college life ended on a very high note. While I was sitting for my final examination there was something going on at the college. The Standard Gauge Railway was about to break ground at the coastal Kenya. Our college was involved in this historical moment being a part of Kenya Railway Corporation.

In our own small way we were to serve at the event hosting His Excellency the President of the Republic of Kenya Uhuru Muigai Kenyatta, Her Excellency the First Lady of the Republic of Kenya Margaret Kenyatta, His Excellency the Vice-President of Kenya William Ruto and several other top government officials.

There was a school choir being formed to perform at the state function. So I had a decision to make about my evenings; to study for my next test or to go for choir practice. The latter was promising me a trip to coastal region for the first time ever.

It would be a great way to finish my college days, I thought. Therefore my decision was easy, I chose to go to coast and run the risk of inadequate preparation for my next exam.

Besides singing is one of my hobbies and I could not miss it for the world.

Most friends thought I was stupid for multitasking during a major examination time. To me it was not only a fun thing to do but also therapeutic. It helped me perform better than those who were studying for straight whole days. I, also from a very early stage taught myself to invest my resources at creating lasting memories.

Just so you know, if you knew about SGR (Standard Gauge Railway) in 2015, 2016, 2017 or even 2018 some of us were at the ground zero and we entertained the president for breaking ground for this historical project. And just so you know I went to Mombasa for the first time in 2013.

This was my first experience after college.

Once again I would go back to my village to strategize for the next move in my life. I was in déjà vu since just a few years earlier I was going back home after completing high school.

The failures and successes of the last transition period were still fresh in my mind. The failed farming venture, the KCSE results and all other events.

One of the defining moments was when I stumbled upon the novel series titled Rangers Apprentice by John Flanagan. It was the first fantasy and adventure novel to read, and also the first novel series.

This book challenged me to become more and become more adventurous in life.

I realized the measure is not how many years you live because you can live one year several times. I realized how beautiful it is to dream and see yourself as you could be. I could not finish reading the entire series because some of the books were missing at the library. Now that I have remembered the educative and entertaining series I might as well buy it all for my library that I am building.

Happy New Year! Here comes 2014; my first year as a college graduate. Welcome to the real life, if you thought life after high school was real, here comes the realest of real.

Since the results of our final exams were not out yet, it was hard to get a job in my field. Thank God I was not asleep on my spare time in college. I had enrolled for electrical installation certification courses commonly known as Wireman Grade Test. I had already done grades 3 & 2 during my 2nd and 3rd years in college.

With this two, I had more than enough qualification than your common day electrician who probably has no certification and if they do just grade 3. Armed with those two certificates and my school's continuous assessment tests transcript, all I wanted was a chance to get back to the city and start hunting for a job.

I had promised myself that I would never tarmac and I knew that when I lay my eyes on an opportunity I will get it.

The only obstacle that stood between me and my new life in the city, Nairobi, was a place to stay. I used to live in the schools hostels before. My only close relative who lived in Nairobi had just relocated back to Meru to start life afresh and pursue their dreams.

I was left in Nairobi alone. My only solution was to ask for accommodation from friends, but most of them just like me were just getting started. I saw the light at the end of the tunnel was my uncle talked to a friend who agreed to host me as I plan to move in by myself and look for a job.

My best friend and brother Elias was more than happy to help me find something to generate some income as we wait for bigger things to come.

He had just started working for a former college-mate who had started a business selling Digital Terrestrial Broadcast Television Decoders during the analog to digital switch off.

My job description was to sell the decoders, configure them, do customer education and sometimes install them for the customer at a cost. This was to earn me Ksh. 7,000 a month.

Not much I know, and yes its Kenyan Shillings not US Dollars or South African Rands.

This to me was better than none: with it I could help my host pay rent, electricity bills and buy food. It is the least one can do for someone who has kindheartedly opened up their door to someone they hardly know.

Working with my friend Elias was a big blessing. He was my mentor and my support system. It was not an easy job especially the part when the pay did not match what we had to go through to get it done. But because of Elias, I stuck with it.

I realized if you have to be in tough situations make sure there is a friend around who will make them lighter on you. Be with someone who will keep your eyes on the bigger picture therefore minding less the hardships of the now.

What made the business tough was the fact that people do not like change. Nobody wants to step out of the norm; of what is already known and accepted as the one and true way. This was evidenced by the long law suits that were going on in our top tier justice apparatus in the country.

The media houses did not want to change and neither did the consumers. These long and uncertain litigations brought a rollercoaster feeling in the minds of the consumers and people were slow wondering if to switch to digital or remain analog.

In other words, there was standstill situation and no product was moving. This was the toughest of times as we were getting paid on the condition that we met our quota.

For several months we were surviving on hope as we were waiting for the final way forward from the justice system. We were victims of people who were fighting change; change that meant good for us; change that would to create more employment and improve mass communication in our motherland.

What do I mean? Fast forward 5 years later, we have television station and radio station for almost each and every part and corner of our diverse country. That means more information to the grass roots, more jobs for the local people, advertisement opportunities for local businesses and promotion of local talents like music to mention but a few.

Next time you are fighting just get out of yourself for a moment and see the bigger picture before you go along the streets ranting. I am just saying.

> *"Intelligence is the ability to accept change."* –
> *Steve Jobs*

Have you ever shared a living space with a friend or a relative where real bills were involved? Where both of you needed to contribute towards something? Have you ever? Do you know what happens if you ever go broke and cannot contribute towards something?

Let me tell you, it gets really weird. It is hard to find the right words to use for this experience; I do not even think there is an English word for it. It happened to me, that is why am, talking about it. During those tough times at my job I found myself unable to contribute towards the bills as agreed with my host. How do you explain to someone that you go to work every day but you are not getting paid?

The answer is you just keep it to yourself and assure them that you would pay up when you get the money. That is what I did and things got weirder.

I remember at one time we ran out of cooking gas and we were to use a kerosene stove. One of my least favorite means of cooking because anytime I spend a minute around it I will surely get a headache. So for a few months a headache in the evening had become the norm.

Sometimes I thought he was punishing me but I could not complain. Never bite the hands that feed you no matter how cruel or dirty they are. I had to keep up with this and a few other weird things that I cannot write here. At this moment, I could not wait to move in by myself. It did not matter how or where, I was done and I was determined to live alone.

Finally I made the move in June 2014. I did not know where I would live. But I knew I would find somewhere. I lived in my friend's workshop, then my employer, for a full week as I looked for a place to start my life.

During all these, Felly was in my life, I did not tell her much of what I was going through but I remember that she used to pay our bills when we met for our occasional dates. She understood that I was underemployed and she was happy to cover up for me.

What a woman, God bless her. Every man could use such a woman in their lives, those that can cover bills when you cannot and not make noise about it. Again am just saying.

About the same time I started my life alone, there came one my most memorable FIFA World Cup Series happening in Rio de Janeiro in Brazil. I call it my most memorable because for the first time in my life I watched the entire soccer action in the comfort of my own humble abode.

Though small, I watched it in a colored television set; my colored television.

Not that I had never watched the FIFA World Cup before. My first time was in the famous 2002 World cup when Ronaldo was every ones favorite. But I watched it on my Dad's 11inch monochrome, Phillips TV set. I also watched the 2010 world cup but in restaurants at a local market.

Due to the nature of the job I was doing, watching television was a must. I would wake up to the tent make up shop; where we displayed our Digital TV decoders, and turn on the television.

I would watch it all day long, only taking commercial breaks with the programs I was following. Thank God I was exposed to the likes of Discovery Channel, Nat Geo, M-Net Movies, Sony Max and all the good little things GOtv had to offer.

After work I would go back to my humble abode and continue watching till late in the night. I watched too much television like if I was compensated for the times that I could not watch back in the village due to limited programs and due to parental control; my parents were the one to give permission on when and how long we could watch our monochrome TV that aired only one channel, KBC.

Looking back I realize that some of the behaviors we develop as adults roots back to our upbringing. We try to rebel the teaching or the demands of our parents to fill that need we had as children.

We sometimes overcompensate and mess our lives because of it. We develop disempowering habits just because we can and just because your mum cannot tell you anything. We do all those things that they said we should not do, all for what?

All for a feeling of control and driving out some sense of authority in our own lives. We take alcohol, smoke and all other destructive habits; mine was too much television.

Days were moving first and reality was kicking into my life faster than before. Around September 2014 I started getting uncomfortable. Uncomfortable because I realized that a whole year was almost coming to an end and I had not achieved anything worthwhile.

All I had was a better knowledge of the hottest TV series, movies and TV programs. All I had was a record time in watching TV in my life so far. All I had was a good looking telecommunication engineering certificate that I knew no plausible way of making it work for me. All I had was a lousy job that paid for my food, rent and utility bills. All I had was a seven day work week with nothing to show for it.

I was stuck and I was in a dangerous comfort zone. Living hand to mouth and not worrying about the dreams that I so much held dear in my heart. Thanks to the delayed digital switch off, I realized I was backpedaling in life.

I was chasing a fantasy that had no promise to change my life as much as it would change my employer's. I was putting my life on hold to live in the shadow of someone else's dream. Of course if the digital switch off happened I could have benefited, but I was not sure it was what I wanted.

There is something that happens in the world of the unseen; spiritual realm, when people get tired of the things as they are and start thinking of how they could be.

Why do I say this?

Because what happened next changed my life for the better and I cannot take credit for it. There are those things that happen for you and you confirm that there must be a God in heaven. This single most occurrence was to shift my thinking and set me up on a totally different course than I thought possible.

And I am reminded of one of my favorite quotes:

> *"Do not conform to the patterns of the world but be ye transformed by the renewing of your mind."*

This shed some light to some of my biggest questions in life and I was definitely transformed.

Before we talk more about this, let us check on my lady Felly. At this point in time, I had already made my intentions known to her. I am not the best when it comes to taking action but I know that I hate the feeling of regret, that feeling of failing.

I would rather do something and fail than live a life of regret full of *what-ifs*. I knew very well that there was a big possibility that she would say no to me but I also knew there was a chance that she liked me as much as I liked her.

I went for the knock-out punch and the results were rather disempowering. We all know that statement that goes like, "Thank you for those nice things you have said about me BUT..."

It was all going well until the demonic BUT came to play. Her BUT was quite absurd and one of the most illogical things I have ever heard.

Taking an analogy of a road trip, her BUT was like not having sun roof on the car you are in.

Taking an analogy of a dining experience, her BUT was like not having an empty plate to put your bones after separating it from your steak.

She said it was good idea to give us a chance, she said I am a great person and anybody would be blessed to date me BUT… she reminded me that she was older than me by six months and sixteen days.

In her belief system the man should be older than the lady in any relationship, even if it is by a day. It made sense in the system of the world but I am a radical; I believe in doing things my way. It did not make any sense to me.

So there I was, six months and sixteen days separating me from the woman of my dreams. I had sought for any possible solution to this but nothing viable came to mind. First it was my desires to show her how mature of a man I was and how much she could count on my word. But I realized I had nothing to prove to her, she knew me better than anyone else.

I even thought of tampering with my birth documents and then come up with a story around it. But then I realized that I did not want to live a lie. I also realized that if someone loves you enough they will handle you as a package including your age.

The final and only solution was not to give up on her. I was determined to help her overlook that itsy-bitsy bit detail about us. She was blowing it out of proportion, and yes it therefore became something huge for her.

Trust me if you put a bacteria under a proper microscope and blow it out of proportion it will look as big as an elephant. I was determined to help her let go off the microscope and let the bacteria be the bacteria that it was.

This is a battle we were to fight for more than a year. We would forget the bacteria for a period of time, but as soon as things got real and close, she would throw her eyes into the microscope and the see the elephant out of the bacteria.

They say love understands; so I did, I did not want to judge her. I understood her and assured her that she had nothing to worry about. With time these efforts became like trying to entertain a goat with a Bohemian Rhapsody Orchestra.

As much as I made sense, both logical and emotional, she did not buy a single bit of it. Talk of being patient. I was patient; they say that good things come to those who wait. What they forgot to add was how long we should wait.

With time these efforts became like trying to entertain a goat with a Bohemian Rhapsody Orchestra.

GREENER PASTURES

Let me take you back to a few moments earlier. I know I did not tell you what happened to me to jumpstart my transformation.

Let us talk about it.

I mentioned that when we start seeing things as they could be and not as they are, coupled with prayer, we put some unseen forces in action that directs us into that vision.

I also said that this helped me answer one of my biggest questions in life. From a very young age I was perturbed by the question of, why are some people poor and others rich and yet there is one God?

Your guess is as good as mine. I never got anyone to answer the question for me. My parents' could not, my Sunday school teacher could not, my priest could not, my school teachers and lecturers could not. But I really desired to get an answer to this question.

I was still in my first job as a sales representative selling digital TV decoders. On this normal day of September 2014 something abnormal was to happen but I had no air of it. Next to my make up shop which was built and brought down every day, there were used books vendors. They had become friends because they were the people I spent most of the day with. They sold mainly school books and a few bibles and dictionaries. I never bothered to take a look at them because I did not imagine finding something worthy of me.

On this particular day, something out of the blue compelled me to go and check out their books as we chat. At that moment in time I was so done with watching television. I just needed something else to do for a change.

As I was going through their books, one caught my eye. It was an old book with a purple tattered cover. I grabbed it and I read, The Cash Flow Quadrant by Robert T. Kiyosaki. It sounded like something a person like me would use and would relate with.

I did what most of us would do, read the content of back cover. Everything I read there I liked and I needed to learn more. So I asked my friend if I could take the book back to my tent shop and take a look at it with intentions to buy if I liked it. Frankly speaking, the buying part was not my intention; I just wanted to create a situation where he would not say no.

Before that day, I thought the people who read books with titles or themes such as how to… or 5 ways to… etcetera, had a mental and/or intellectual and/or emotional problem and as part of their therapy, the books were recommended to them.

So how could I spend money on a book that should be recommended by a therapist? I used to read books but only novels with interesting stories, not boring financial education books like the cash flow quadrant.

I read the preface of the book and I loved the kind of radical attitude of the author. He definitely saw things different from the rest of the vast majority and I saw myself in him. At that juncture I rushed out to my friend to ask how much he would sell the book to me.

I was surprised when he said he would sell it at Ksh. 200. To me that was a lot of money. Being a typical Kenyan; where we bargain for everything, I said I had Ksh. 100. To my surprise he said he would take that. To my bigger surprise I realized I was not willing to give even the Ksh. 100. I gave an excuse why I could not pay right away and promised to get back to him in the course of the day.

My task was to read as much pages of the book as possible to prove if it was worth my Ksh. 100.
Reading it I did; after the first chapter I got up slowly took Ksh. 100 to the book vendor and got back without looking back just in case he changed his mind.

A few minutes earlier I saw this book worthless but now I was ready to pay more than 5 times that he asked me to. It was really heaven sent. In the first few pages it answered my lifelong question of why are some people poor and others rich despite having one creator.

I was getting a world class teaching on finances and more importantly economic practices that we engage in to earn money. The latter in turn determines our means of livelihood therefore our wealth or our poverty. My answer came in as a puzzle and I had to piece it together.

He talked about assets and liabilities, working for money and money working for you, getting employed and creating employment, income statement and balance sheet to mention but a few.

Then my answer came to me that the reason why some people are rich and others poor despite having the same creator is their mindset. The secret was totally between the ears. The secret was not in how much education, which family we were born in, your social status, your surname, or even your spirituality and/or religion. The secrets were only between the ears.

At this moment it started to make sense why Paul told the Romans to not conform to the patterns of this world but be transformed by renewing their minds; by questioning their beliefs, thinking and seeking the truth that would set them free.

The cash flow quadrant disrupted my thinking and made me see things in a totally different light. I realized that the rich people do not work for money, they instead seek to solve problems and sooner rather than later money would follow them and indeed work for them as they focus on doing their work; solving problems.

The poor on the other side trade their time for money, meaning they work for money. This was so radical for me; I never saw it like that before. But I now did, I started getting a picture of what I wanted to do with my life. I definitely wanted to become a problem solver and let money work for me.

The book also talked about how the rich and the poor spend their money. The rich use their money to buy assets and the poor use their money to buy liabilities. It then defined liabilities as something that takes money out of your pockets and assets as something that brings money into your pockets.

Wow! This was a totally new concept that my business studies teachers forgot to mention. The next lesson was how the poor use money before earning it and therefore living in debts all their lives. The rich only spend the surplus of their earning; meaning they have a finance management tool like use of financial income statements and balance sheets.

The most eye opening was the quadrant itself. It explained the four quadrants on which everyone who earns is located. There was Employee Quadrant, the Self-employed Quadrant, the Business owner Quadrant and the Investor Quadrant.

The first quadrant, being an employee was said to be where most people are and where the current school system is leading people to. It was mentioned that on this quadrant, people trade their time for money, they value phantom security in the name of job security, and they save in retirement plans hoping to get rich through them and several other unpleasant things.

The second quadrant, self-employment are said to be the people who believe that if you want things done well, do them yourself. These are mainly the professional in specific areas, from plumbers to doctors. People who have started their business with them as the center piece of operation. This is mostly seen as a better option than being employed but in the real sense, the only difference is that the former owns the job.

They also trade time for money, if they close shop, the business goes with them. Because of this most self-employed people have to work harder and longer to keep the plates spinning. Their lifestyle is quite limited on how much they can do besides their small business. They just cannot afford to be away for even a minute.

Moving on to the third quadrant, we meet the Business owner. Unlike the self-employed lawyer, the business owner decided to start a business that does not have to rely on him for its operation. They open shop, and instead of being the rock star, they become a coach to a team of lieutenants who go out there and represent the company's clients in the legal matters.

With time this person will have built a strong team of advocates better than themselves and they have a business system that can run with or without them. Because of the money the company is able to generate as a result of a great business system, the owners can hire even more talented people to expand the capacity of the company. Then they can afford to go for 6 month vacations twice a year. They have a money bearing tree; their business system.

Last is the investor quadrant, where money goes into work for you in different vehicles of investment. In this quadrant we talk of ROI, (returns on investment) capital gains, interest rates, stocks, bonds, IPOs etc. This is where the wealth is made and/or multiplied. Most business owners put their earning in investment plans like stocks, valuable commodities, real estate and many more.

With the distinction of the four quadrants I realized why we have the rich and the poor; the people of little or no means to provide for necessities and people with abundance of means to provide for the necessities. I wanted to be in the latter, having been raised in the former and having not liked it, I wanted to be wealthy and have abundance and Robert Kiyosaki through his book The Cash Flow Quadrant hinted on what I should and should not do. Now you understand when I say that this book set me on a different course in my life.

After reading the book it was unthinkable to remain comfortable in my comfort zone. I started reaching out to friends and colleagues at my former place of attachment asking for a chance to be of help to them. After several chats I got a chance to serve with my former colleagues. I was doing it pro bono with efforts to show my commitment to anyone who might need me in their team. More importantly I wanted to be in action towards achieving bigger goals in my life.

That was a beginning of something awesome. After my first volunteer work, I got a chance to work for the company I volunteered to for a two weeks contract. I was officially out of the salesman job and I was officially into my profession: a telecommunication engineer.

After that job, I was referred to another company that was to be my next employer; little did I know. It all started as a contractual job that I did from October to December 2014. Within that short period I was able to get a chance to travel around the country especially the western part. On top of that I had proved myself worth of employment in the company, not by interview but by merit. Come January the next year I knew for sure I would get a job with the company.

This was to be a greener pasture for me and I was excited about it.

Robert Kiyosaki came to my life to stir things up and take me out of my comfort zone. I did not practice all that he taught to the best of my interest because I was looking to be into the worst of the quadrants. But deep down I knew it was a new beginning and my life was to change for the better. In order to step into the Business owner quadrant that I so much desired to be in, I needed to start here, get a job.

My plan was to get into the telecommunication industry, gain as much experience as possible, network with people and go start my own thing hoping to build a business system instead of just being self-employed. I had a dream. I had a dream to build the leading telecommunication firm in Meru County.

With the devolved government system I knew it would have been a wise idea to devolve such services to my home county. This was The Amerucan Dream version 1.0. It was not clearly cut out on how I would make it happen but I knew I would learn as time goes by.

Let us come back to my new job. It was quite interesting to not give it some airtime. After the New Year's celebration, it was a marathon in the service industry to get businesses ready to start off the New Year on a high note.

At the time we had a project for networking for a new office building of a leading cleaning company. This kept me busy for the first half of the month. I had not gotten the job yet, at least not officially. Around mid-January we sat down with my boss to discuss my employment terms and formalize things. It was an exciting moment, first I was getting a job without an interview and secondly I could say that I now had a decent job.

My excitement was great but not so long lasting as I would have wanted it to be. Robert Kiyosaki was right about employment; for a moment I stopped to think to myself, what was I getting into? Why? Because my salary could not get to half what I thought it would be.

Since college I thought or was told the minimum salary for a technician of my qualifications in an entry job was at least Ksh. 50,000. When my employer asked for my expected pay I quoted the latter. To my surprise he almost chocked on the tea we were talking while negotiating my salary. He later made the most heart breaking statement. He said, "Frank, we are a young company, we have a few technicians most of whom have been here since we started and none of them is near earning that much". In other words, I was being too ambitious and unrealistic. So I called on him to make his offer.

He said, "Coming to this meeting I had Ksh. 15,000 in mind but since I can see your ambition and commitment to grow, the best we can pay you is Ksh. 19,500." "What happens next?" I asked. "We will be reviewing your performance every 3 months and a salary increment done accordingly" he replied.

This was a 'take it or leave it' deal, it was final and he had no room for negotiation. I had a decision to make, and it was easy, my last job was not paying half of that amount, this was much better. I took it, hoping to go up the corporate ladder and maybe soon I would get to where I wanted to start. I know many people who graduated with high hopes of a well-paying job. But as soon as life paid them with a reality check, they settled for anything.

That is one of the reasons I have a grudge on the kind of education we are struggling too hard to get. In Kenya alone, we have more than 75,000 new employment seekers every year.

Young Kenyans who have been sold a lie of a beautiful corporate dream coming true after getting good grades.

Young Kenyans with no real life skills to use on their day to day life but with papers that will supposedly make their dreams come true.

Young Kenyans who cannot think creatively and innovatively to create employment instead of seeking for some.

Young Kenyans who have not been sold on the importance of taking risks while young enough and dream big.

Young Kenyans who were conditioned that they should never make mistakes by the way they handled mistakes in school because they were taming you for employment.

Just think with me for a minute, what was the purpose of punishing you for making noise in class? To make you better person? I do not think so. To make you pass your tests better? To help you grasp the class teachings? Not at all!

The concept is, come in here (school) on stipulated time, sit down where you have been allocated, when you have something to say, ask for permission by raising your hand and if you want to answer biological call, ask for permission too.

Now compare that to what happens in the work place. You are given the time lines to work, they even have invested a chunk of money into a system that will clock you in and clock you out every day so that you do not lie about your time at work. Some have gone to an extent of counting the number of times you use the bathroom. Then they tell you what to do and you are not allowed to question it. You have to ask for permission to go tend for a personal emergency. They punish you for any mistake you do either by getting memos, warnings, pay cut, and demotion and sometimes you might even lose your job.

Do you not see a similarity between our work places and our schools? Is it correct if we say they were made for each other? Meaning the school system, with an exception of very few, was made to deliver ready servants who can easily follow rules and do what they are told without questioning. Would that not be right? Can we say that the majority of the school system kills our human nature of being creative, innovative and progressive reducing us to nothing but slaves and addicts to a system that cannot take care of us all? Do not get me wrong, I love education I just hate the way it is structured and delivered.

"If you judge the success of a fish by its ability to climb a tree it will spend its entire life thinking that it's a failure." –Albert Einstein

---

Now I had a new job, not with the terms I expected but it was a nice start. I knew I was a hard worker and with no time I would scale up the corporate ladder and be the best in the company.

We went to work, being a fast learner nothing seemed to stop me in the operation of the company. Of course there is hardly anything I learnt in class that was applicable directly to the field. It was like going to a whole new class and starting over. And it leaves me wondering why we are interviewed on academic staff in the first place. Anyway I do not want the answer to that question because I will never sit in such an interview and if I ever employ people I will do a different kind of interview.

Three months after signing the contract came in quick. I was promised a quarterly appraisal that would be accompanied by a salary increment if I performed. I was sure of my industrious spirit and I was the one asking for an appraisal. I do not remember what really happened but I remember begging for it for more than two months. Instead of it coming after three months it came after six months.

Those to me were three months with no better pay. I was angry about but I could not do anything to change it. That is when you know that there is a difference between your dream and your employer's.

Fast forward a week after the appraisal, it was around pay day and I was highly expectant of what was to come. I knew it would be a handsome amount and I would go smiling all the way to the bank. I could not believe my eyes when I saw that my raise was Ksh. 2000. That was a surprise, I thought I had given the company more and I was hoping for more.

There and then Robert Kiyosaki voice with the words written on the cash flow quadrant book started playing in my head. There I was proving all that he had taught me a few months ago.

Then I remembered where I was hoping to start, at least Ksh. 50,000. Then I realized with this rate of growth I would take not less than ten years of my life to get where I wanted to start in the first place. Then I would take some more ten more years to reach at the top of the corporate ladder.

I did not like that idea; I realized I signed me a low deal. Yes I am ambitious, and because of that I have gotten into many troubles that I will mention later. I am just saying because I can feel someone saying in their mind, *these youths of nowadays do not have patience; they want to get rich quick*. And for the record, the middle class is no longer the people earning $1,000 a month in developing countries; millionaire is the new middle class. Yes we do not have time to be miserable in a world where you can be anything.

At that time I started asking myself some quality questions and I urgently needed the answers. I started following Robert Kiyosaki in all platforms that he was in. I realized I had started getting comfortable again and I needed a kick to get me off the couch.

From his book "The Cash Flow Quadrant" he had recommended a few books and one of them was "Think and Grow Rich." I was able to get an e-book online and I started reading it. As I was devouring the wisdom of one of the greatest authors of the last century, Robert sent me another e-book as a gift on email. The book was entitled "The Business of The 21st Century." This was a must after "Think and Grow Rich."

Before I forget, I highly recommend the three books to anyone seeking to pursue personal education.

Think and grow rich really messed me up, it disrupted what I thought riches are and what I thought success is about. It dived deeper into why we should focus on what goes on between our ears in any endeavor. It introduced me to human psychology and how our brains work.

With evidence from the history, it showed how notable people consciously created the circumstances they wanted by utilizing things we all have at our disposal. It taught me how to focus my wishes into a burning desire to go for the things I want. It taught me how to employ visualization and imagination to see clearly how things could be. It taught me how to develop my faith muscle as the single most powerful state to achieve anything. It taught me to have positive self-talk and empower myself with the words I say to myself and many more things that all work together to create lasting and fulfilling success.

From the past centuries the book was full of examples of people who used those simple but profound and rarely heard of secrets to create the success which the world recognizes them for. It featured people from the father of the motor car Henry Ford, to the famous inventor Thomas A. Edison, to the founding fathers of American democracy.

They were all valid examples to emulate and "Think and Grow Rich" became one of my favorite books. Since then I read it at least once per year. It is the most recommended book by more than 80% of top CEOs and Entrepreneurs. It has been read by leading preachers, lawyers, presidents, doctors, moms, and people from all walks of life. It is a book for everyone. If you do not get anything else from this book at least go buy yourself "Think and Grow Rich", thank me later.

After reading "Think and Grow Rich" I was totally sold into self-development and I was ready to read and practice anything that made sense to me. "Think and Grow Rich" had recommended that I should get a mastermind group or build one.

Building one was the easiest way and I started looking for people who can mentor me and people who had achieved all that I wanted to achieve. This is usually the time you come to a realization of the kind of people you have been allowing into your life.

I looked around diligently, seeking from all corners of my prior interactions. Everybody I ever admired was put into the list. Now the moment of truth came when I sat down to narrow down to who could mentor me on what. Shock on me, there was hardly anyone who qualified to really guide me in the areas I valued most.

The only person I left on the list was one; the General Manager of the cleaning company I mentioned earlier. I reached out to her but she was unavailable to commit to such a role. So I moved on and continued to reach out to people whom I thought could become good mentors.

I realized that we have a shortage of people to look up to. An average person who is my age knows less than three people who they can count on for mentorship beside their family members. And those that know three, two of them are inaccessible to them and the other can only be counted on in one or two areas of life.

Disclaimer, I am talking from personal experience not from a professional research. But I dare you to ask anyone less than 30 years old how many people are in their circle and can be counted on for mentorship.

Out of frustration of trying to find people who have achieved exceptional results in their lives, I turned on to my best friend of the time; Google. I searched for the leading thought leaders in several aspects of life and followed their social media accounts especially on YouTube.

About the same time I started reading Robert Kiyosaki's book "The Business of the 21st Century." It was yet another eye opener; the first was general streams of income but this was about business.

To give you a sneak peek into the book for those who will not read the book despite my recommendation, I will highlight what I learnt. First, I thought any business was an awesome business as long as you were passionate about it. But Robert Kiyosaki was able to help me distinguish between different business models. He also highlighted the pros and cons of them all.

One of the most outstanding comments he made is that irrespective of the success he has achieved in the business he still does not have enough to build a successful business from scratch all by himself. No one can do it and neither should you think that you can.

What he meant was, to keep the plates spinning in any business, there are many skills required. Accounting is required, administration, management, production, human resource, customer service, sales and marketing, social media strategists etc. Most self-employed people try to do it all and end up being jacks of all trades instead of focusing on what they are good at. This is where the concept of building business like a system comes to play.

Think of a successful business like a sports car from the top brands, for example my favorite Nissan GTR. The car moves as one but it has many things going for it in-order to get the outward results. It has an engine that sends 650horse power to the wheels, by the help of a sophisticated transmission, utilizing the principle of fuel air and fire; made possible by the electrical system that pumps the fuel, and provides the spark etc.

As you can see this is how a big business operates. I am insisting on this because I know Kenyans are sold out on self-employment. Also it is my dream that we all think beyond employing ourselves and create more jobs for the desperate majority who will never do anything with their lives if they never get a job.

The book continued to explain why it is important for all people to develop the leadership skills that are necessary to make the Nissan GTR in form of a business run smoothly. Most people shy away from trusting people with their business because they have no idea of how to handle people; zero people skills. And Robert emphasizes developing such skills.

In solution to all these problems he brought to lame light, he encourages all people who wish to make any success in business to join a network marketing company. He refers to a typical network marketing as a school for entrepreneurs.

Why?

From his explanation he highlighted that a good network marketing company, (meaning there are bad ones Ha-ha!) is focused on training its business associates in a way to grow them instead of exploiting them as experienced in traditional corporate world. He said that network marketing offers an on job learning that you cannot get from any business school. He mentioned that the skills gotten from the network marketing business could be applied in any entrepreneurial venture with greater success than those of MBAs.

The peoples skills, the sales and marketing skills, the networking skills, the customer service skills, the leadership skills, the communication and public speaking skills, event planning and organizing skills, presentation skills and many more.

When I saw all the promises laid out by Robert in his book I was already sold out to getting into a network marketing company to at least get the training promised. These were all the skills I needed to learn from the mentors I was looking for. I had made a breakthrough in my search for people to mentor me; Robert Kiyosaki just came through for me one more time. I really pray that I meet him in person and say THANK YOU while we are still in this world. Till then God bless him.

I made decision to learn more about the Network Marketing Industry which Robert Kiyosaki refers to as the business of the twenty first century and definitely be part of it. Who makes such a life changing decision by reading from a Japanese American old man who does not know them?

Frank does, I can do that anytime. For your information some of the people who have had the greatest impact in my life are people from the other corners of the globe. People I do not know; people who do not even know I exist. You just met one, many more are coming in this book or somewhere else; you will meet them. I call them my tele-mentors.

From September 2015 when I read the book, I took my time to do all the research I could to get an impartial view of the industry that most Kenyans either know little about or are completely wrong about. So I could not rely on consulting people I knew. Apparently everyone except me knew someone if not themselves who failed terribly at the business. What they meant was Robert Kiyosaki was wrong and out of his mind to recommend the business. Your guess is as good as mine; I did not trust them, so I went with Robert's verdict and switched the negative noises off.

I learnt that in the U.S.A the network marketing business was a huge thing. Research had it that at least one person in every family is involved in the industry in one way or another. No wonder Robert said that if he were to start over he would build a network marketing business instead of the traditional business. It was credited to have created more millionaires than several other industries combined. It was definitely working in the U.S.A and that is all I needed to make the decision.

Do not forget I still had a job going on. I was to pursue this business opportunity part time just like Robert advices. I use to wake up very early in the morning and get to the office before anyone else so that I can have my personal study and research time before 8am.

In September 2015 I learnt a lot between 6am to 8am than most people do in a whole year. The power of part time; I hear the biggest corporate giants started as a side thing for the founders.

In October, I chose the company to join on a simple criterion. It had to be American, over 50 years in operation, in nutrition and wellness, with a likable mission statement and was operating in Kenya. My choice was easy; I would love to make it known to you all but for the purpose of this book I will keep it to myself. I loved their mission statement which was by then, People Empowering People. I wanted to be empowered and this was definitely the best place for me to be.

In November 2015 I was in Network Marketing officially and I could brag about having a side hustle. When my colleagues had nothing to do with their spare time, I was busy mastering a new skill or getting to understand the basics of human nutrition. On weekends I was busy doing business meetings and attending events. I was hungry for knowledge and I went all out to get it. I took notes and even made a budget to buy self-help books.

At work I was becoming a better employee because of the personal development I was experiencing from my side hustle. I was growing into something better and everyone noticed it. I was onto something and I was not looking back. My life had started accelerating on a trajectory I set out on a year ago and it was all that I wanted.

I read a book by Dr. Norman Vincent Peale, "The Power of Positive Thinking." I later learnt he was the pastor who ministered to the current POTUS Donald Trump as he was growing up. Trump himself admitted that it is Dr. Vincent who laid a foundation of the success he has now achieved. Getting a privilege to read from the same person who impacted the life of now a billionaire and the most powerful president in the world was a blessing.

At that time I learnt something profound. That we might never get to learn from the people we admire but we can read their books or even better read the books that they read so that we can know what they already know. Then it will be just a matter of time and we will be like them or better than them.

I became a voracious reader of any book that was recommended at out training in my Network Marketing business or from any other person that I followed. I literally became a personal development junkie; on commute I was either reading a book or listening to a speech or an audio book. At home I was watching speeches from my tele-mentors; Robert Kiyosaki, Les

Brown who is one of my closest, Grant Cardone, Jim Rohn and Earl Nothingale.

The year 2016 came in quick and I was also growing at a quick pace. My mindset was given over haul maintenance by the material I consumed. More and more I proved how much garbage I was fed in school. I experienced firsthand what education should be like. But at this moment I was still a student and I was focused more into learning and practicing than trying to help the world understand that there was a better way.

In 2016 my salary had gone up a notch higher, it was around Ksh. 24,000. I told you it would take me ten years to get to fifty thousand that I was hoping to start with. I am glad I started looking and seeking for ways and means to become more and do more while I still could.

I am not a fan of blowing my own trumpet but most people disregard the signs until it is too late. They realize that their jobs cannot meet their dreams when they are already behind on their bills. Not that I never missed signs, I have missed them but out of ignorance. I missed the signs Felly was giving me and it really hit me between the legs.

CHAPTER 6

EPIPHANY

While I was gaining so much information that had so much power to transform my life, I was stuck. I wanted to bring the people I cared about with me. Especially Felly; she was part of my bigger plan of a better life and I did not want to leave her behind. I tried using my newly learnt philosophies about life to help her get off the line of our age difference and focus on building our future. But it was all in vain. And when I say I tried just know that for sure I tried.

One of the most hurting signs she gave me was in early 2016. There was the famous Safaricom 7's at Kasarani International Stadium and I proposed that we should go and have fun over there. Yes she agreed. But on the condition that when I buy the tickets I should also buy one for her sister. My plan was to have our lone moment but her wish was my command. Besides it does not hurt to spend some time with a prospective sister-in-law. I cheerfully bought three tickets on Thursday and made sure that I had no other commitment on the coming Saturday. It would be our first day to go outdoors and have fun. I was excited about it and I had a plan to make it memorable.

The game day came, early in the morning I texted her and reminded her that it was the day. I proposed we meet at 12noon so that we make it to the stadium by 2pm when the first match was kicking off. She gladly accepted.

I made all the preparations I could make waiting for the time to leave and have a moment of my life. I always make an effort to get to my meetings early. I was at ground zero at 11:30am and I texted her to let her know that I was waiting, no reply. I was not alarmed it was still early. At 12noon, I called and no answer!

12:15pm I called twice, still no answer. 12:30pm with a little bit of frustration, I called 3 times, still no answer. At this moment I had to be generous with my words. I sent her a text that was as long as texts could get trying to display my disappointment and my hurt. She did not reply that too.

I have never gone short of the grace to give people benefits of doubt. I assumed that she was caught up with something or may be already on her way. So I talked myself to wait till 1pm.

Waiting I did, but she did not have the courtesy of contacting me to tell me what was going on. At 1:15pm I realized I was all by myself and I better get moving to practice some self-love with my three tickets. Being the good person that I am or may be the stupid person that I am, (sometimes it is hard to distinguish between being good and being stupid) I did not leave until it was 1:30pm. I called for one last time and now I confirmed that no one is showing up.

I was tempted to call some friends and donate the tickets to them and at least massage my molested ego. But, I choose not to lie to my friends and I chose to learn my lesson the hard way. At the entrance I met a middle-aged lady who came to the stadium thinking there was no entrance fee, she was about to be sent out by the security guard but I came to her rescue. I donated one of the three tickets to her. I had no time to see the joy in her but I know she was happy and thankful. All I wanted at that time was to have a great time at the rugby tournament and forget my "dada issues".

At this point in time I had not decided what to do with Felly but I knew it would never be the same. She had betrayed my trust in her and it was going to take more than an apology to get it back.

What do you so when you are heartbroken and in midst of a wild crowd having fun and cheering for their favorite rugby team? You join them! I made friends, took my problems and zipped them in my wallet and had great wild fun with friends that we never got to know each other's name. It was a great experience but of course it could have been better if it went according to plan.

At 6pm the tournament was terminated for the night to continue the next day. On my way home, I decided to pass by one of the restaurants we frequently met with Felly to take a cup of tea as I was really hungry. I also needed some time to replay the events of the day and devise the way forward.

Little did I know what was waiting for me inside as I made the decision to go take some tea? The first face to see was the one and only her Royal Highness Felly in all her grace and beauty. I cannot tell if she was shocked to see me or not but she seemed disturbed. In her company was a man I knew from college, I can call him a friend. Actually he is the guy who showed me around on my first day in college. I did not even know that they knew each other. I was surprised and curious. What was going on here?

Some part of me wanted to walk away and get my own table but the male in me wanted to sit down there where they were and get to understand why I was stood up and she was there with another man. When she asked me to share the table with them I gladly accepted. At least I would achieve my agenda without intruding their space.

I sat there hoping she would become apologetic and explain what happened. But she did not all she asked what I would use. At that moment in time the appetite I had was long gone and I could not mouth anything heavier that water. My mouth was dry out of frustration and hurt and water is all I needed.

I sat there looking at her unapologetic posture wondering what she thought I was. Finally she got the nerve to ask me how the rugby tournament was. Thanks to my calmness, I did not create a scene as much as deep inside I wanted to let the world know that I was hurt. I took a few deep breaths and regained my full composure, trying to be as understanding as I could. I said, "Before I tell you about the tournament, tell me why the hell I had to attend it alone despite our prior plans?"

I do not quite remember what her answer was but I am as sure as death and taxes that it was all manure. It was some excuses in the range of being caught up with house chores. "And then what the heck are you doing with this man here if you had such a busy day?" I almost asked but good manners refused to let me. I could not sit there and be lied to while I struggled to figure out what the truth was. I excused myself against her will and left them. As I walked away I knew my relationship with Felly would never be the same and I decided to do whatever it took to forget her.

On that day for the first time in my life I bought myself some alcohol. It was that bad. On my way home I passed by a bar and bought myself two Smirnoff Ice with Guarana. Being a teetotaler that was enough to get me high and sleep without thinking about the worst of the days in my life.

It was the first time I was really hurt badly; the type of hurt you feel as if someone drove a two-edged sword into your heart, spun 180 degrees anti-clockwise and pulled it back. I used to wonder why men turned to alcohol when they had some serious "dada issues". On that day I was on the receiving end, I got into their shoes.

I definitely do not think that alcohol is a solution to any problem and especially not emotional problems but I will never be quick to judge those who take it for the sake of trying to ease pain. May be if they knew better they would do better.

The next day was the day for me to know better. I sat myself down and asked; why I am hurt by actions of a lady who has proven that they do not respect me? I did not get an answer, unfortunately. I asked why did I let Felly get into my head to the point of breaking my personal principles and took alcohol in the name of "she hurt me"? Again I did not get an answer, but one thing was clear, if she really cared about me she could have treated me better.

One more thing was clear, that Felly was to be loved from a distance and that I would let her be. Besides for the longest time she has been trying to prove to me why our relationship could not work into something worthwhile.

It would take a while before I forgot her but I was determined to do it. A year is more than enough to know if you are headed somewhere with someone with whom you are involved with. We were almost two years in; it was definitely time for both of us to move on.

Besides my *"wendo issues"* things were working well in other areas of my life. My personal development journey was in a momentum. Actually it is because of the active self-development I was pursuing that I was able to forgive and forget Felly's shortcomings. It happened so fast that for a moment I thought I was pretending to have forgiven and let her go.

My network marketing business was grooming me up so well. I had met some great people some of whom became my friends and customers for my products. At work I was doing my best to be of the greatest service to my employer. The company was growing and I was happy to be a part of the team making it possible. Things were happening and as they were happening some would come to affect my life more than I ever thought possible.

My employer announced that we might get an opportunity to work on some third party contract for the UN in Somalia Republic. Great news for sure but we were not so much psyched by them. We know how disturbed our neighboring country has been for the years and still is. No one was in a rush to speak in a manner suggesting that they would go for the Somalia job let alone agreeing to it. I realized everyone was freaked out about it, I saw an opportunity.

"Opportunity dances with those already on the dance floor." - Anonymous

---

The requirement was to get a passport in the shortest time possible as we wait for the confirmation of the contracts. It was around May 2016; I was determined to land this uncompetitive opportunity to play the hero of the employer company. I made the arrangements and got my passport. If I never use it for Somalia at least I have it handy for wherever it might be needed.

At this point in time I had also taken a few steps towards building a better life that my personal growth endeavors promised. Part of what I learnt from Robert Kiyosaki was to develop a savings culture. On every pay day I would set aside at least ten percent of my earnings and saved them in co-operative society that I had joined back in September 2015.

Another thing I learnt from Robert Kiyosaki was that if someone desires to be wealthy and stay wealthy they needed to put strategies to protect their wealth. Part of protecting the wealth he advised to get rid of people who might so much rely on you financially by empowering them. Empowering them to create something they can call their own and have a lifelong steady source of income. He was definitely talking about family.

So my plan was to help my parents start up a sustainable and decent business that would cater for all their needs without necessarily relying on me or any of my siblings. This was my priority and the savings I was putting together was aimed to making this dream come true. As a result I really had to sacrifice my comfort and gratification to save up more money.

I lived in a house I did not like to live in, but I knew the end result was worth the sacrifice. I could not buy the clothes that I wanted to buy or the shoes that I liked. I love gadgets, I could not buy them either since I had a goal larger than self.

This started in September to October of 2015. The plan was simple, save enough money that if I took a loan three times my savings I would get enough capital to jump start a project. On the project selection I had to choose something that no matter what may come, it will be profitable at the end of it all. My choice was simple; I have always admired and been passionate about decent and spacious living spaces. Having been brought up in the rural parts of Meru in a small semi-permanent house and then coming to the city to see big better houses, I knew what I was brought up in was not enough.

I had seen houses with big bathrooms than my bedroom back in the countryside. I had seen houses with big kitchen than the sitting room of our rural house. I had experienced the sense of fulfillment that comes with living in a spacious house.

Back in our village as I had mentioned earlier, the main building material is wood cut from *Mukima* tree. This was used to replace the traditional mud houses that were thatched using straw for the roof. I had a privilege to see such a house that belonged to my late great grandma who left us when I was in high school.

To my village standards, a timber house was a great house. But things are changing; somehow despite treating the timber for building mites other insects have found ways to damage the wood. This vice has become so serious and almost uncontrollable. The insects are getting wiser than the humans and the integrity of the house structures compromised.

The alternative would have been to use quarry stones to build permanent houses. Unfortunately, that is an expensive building technology that neither my parents nor most of the villagers afford. When I was growing up permanent stone and mortar houses were mainly built by teachers or other white collar employees whom were rare.

Here I saw an opportunity; most people wanted a bigger better house but the problem was affordability. If nobody did, at least I was sure my parents wanted and needed a better house.

A few years ago I had heard of a building technology that cuts off the building costs by up to fifty percent. This was possible because unlike the traditional stone or brick building, the technology did not require mortar to join the walls together. If you know anything about construction you will bear me witness that cement is one of the most costly items in the whole deal. And that also means that mortar is the most expensive raw material that goes into creating a decent house.

This technology was promising to cut off the mortar in a handsome way. Why? The technology relies on blocks made from soil that can be dug on the construction site. Also the blocks are made in such a way that they interlock with each other, making a solid wall without being joined with mortar. Also the walls made from the blocks were so smooth that they did not need any plastering for aesthetic purpose. Now you understand why the costs can be reduced by up to fifty percent.

This was an interesting idea and I saw it was the best fit for the project I wanted to launch for my parents. This was a dream come true; I had always wanted to build my parents a house and now this idea I would do more than that, I would also build them a business.

For the longest time my dad has been a handy man, he knows how to use his tools and his hands to make functional structures. I knew he was a natural when it comes to building and construction. The business would have him and with his skills he would make it work. I was so confident on that.

The plan was to buy the machine that is used to make the interlocking soil blocks. With the help of my co-operative society I would make that a reality. Secondly, we would gather our efforts together (me and my parents) and build a house. This house was to serve as a tool for marketing our new found building technology to the rest of the villagers and beyond.

The worst case scenario was that my parents would get a new house. Not just a new house but a spanking beautiful and unique permanent house. So I was at peace, even if we never got to turn this into a business, they would have a house. Nothing could go wrong beyond that.

To be sure about it, one day I went home and sat my mum and dad down and we had a chat. I declared my commitment to helping them start a decent business that would serve them all the way without ever relying on us. I asked if my idea was good enough or would they rather invest in dairy farming. They both strongly agreed with me that my idea was on point because the worst case scenario was that they would have a house out of it. We agreed on that and I went to work. They even suggested helping in raising the funds. This was a home run and more than ever I was obsessed in making it a reality. By August 2016, this would be a done deal; it was just but a matter of time.

"Wisdom is the principle thing; therefore get wisdom: and in all thy getting, get understanding."
Proverbs 4:7 [KJV]

At work, the Somalia jobs were coming to a reality. On July 7th 2016 (nobody forgets the exact date they first boarded an airplane and the first day they left their country) I flew out of the country, Kenya, to the neighboring Somalia for site survey. It was also the first day to carry dollar bills in my wallet. It was such a great feeling and I loved every bit of it.

Of course just like most people on their first flight I was at the Airport at 4am for a flight that was to be boarded at 7:15am.

Thank you to the several movies I had watched prior to my first flight I acted like a "pro flier". I knew what most of the things meant and what I was required to do when and how. I must have anticipated the actions to take when boarding and boarding the plane but I had no idea how it felt to fly. With all the physics I had learnt so far; the Bernoulli's Principle and the airfoil theorem, I still had my doubts that a jet aircraft would really take off and fly. Well until it took off, ascending more than 35,000 ft. above the sea level and well past the white clouds.

There I was flying for the first time. I am sure that I was the first person in my family (on my dad and mum's sides) to fly out of the country. I might need to confirm this just to make sure, but whatever I find out, just know I was the first person to fly abroad in our family. And I think I am still the only one who had flown out. May be we dive deeper into the distant relatives to find a number two.

An hour later we landed at Aden Abdulle International Airport in Mogadishu. I was on transit so I did not get a chance to get out of the plane. My destination was Egal International Airport in Hargeisa Somaliland.

Somaliland is the most developed state of Somalia Republic that fought the Al Shaabab insurgents' way before they became an international concern. It is the most peaceful place to be in the whole of Somalia. That gave me a peace of mind but it did not fully eliminate the fear that the plane could be shot from the skies by the militants. My movies served me well but they also reminded me of things like rocket launchers than can be used by terrorists to shoot planes from the ground. Anyway we landed safely at Egal International Airport.

I forgot to mention that everyone who cared about me had strongly advised me not to go to Somalia. I was acting against everyone's will but the experience I got no amount of money could buy that. They were advising me not to go because of the potential risk involved.

But to me they were telling me to say no to my first time in an airplane, my first time out of the country and into a foreign country and culture. They were telling me to say no to adventure and the experience of a lifetime. One thing I am as sure as a stone falls from the hand that lets go, is I could not be writing this book if I did not go to Somalia. Stick around, you will find out why.

At Hargeisa, I took the least time possible to complete my work and then spent the rest of my time having fun over there. For the first time I spent my time in a 3 Star Hotel, Ambassador Hotel. Frankly speaking it was my first time to spend a night in any hotel. I was privileged to do what I saw in movies: room service. How can you stay in a 3 star hotel and not call for room service? On top of that it was my first time to eat the Italian delicacy, lasagna. First times are a great thing for me and I rarely forget them so bear with me.

To cut the long story short, Hargeisa was fun and I would highly recommend it if you ever want to visit the country. The people of Hargeisa are also very welcoming and courteous to the visitors. I did not mind coming back to do the job that brought me for the site survey.

The work commenced less than a month later and I spent more than 3 weeks in Hargeisa Somaliland. I made friends and created memories that I will forever be thankful for.

"If you never travel, you will always think that your mother is the best cook."

The second flight, which came before the second visit to Hargeisa, was to another state of Somali called Puntland. Garowe is the main town of the state and that is where I was going for another site survey at the UN mission in Somalia offices. Unlike Somaliland, Puntland was quite scary because it was at the heart of the Al Shaabab militant stronghold. The main Garowe airport was undergoing construction and we had to use an alternative airstrip, Conoco Airport; that was in the outskirts of Garowe Township.

I got the full intensity of the matters around here when we were given bullet proof vests to wear and then board heavily armored UN vehicles that were to take us into Garowe. We also had an escort of local armed forces who were heavily armed with automatic weapons and a pickup truck with a ginormous machine gun mounted on it. I was scared off my wits but I loved the adrenaline rush. It felt like I was in the midst of a scene extracted from the Strike Back TV series.

I liked the way the big motorcade sped its way into the town and the prowess of the drivers. This was a real life event that felt like a movie to me. I did not imagine there was such a reality to any person alive on earth but there I was, less than 2 hours from my mother land.

Garowe visit was fruitful, I met a few fellow countrymen who were working in Garowe and they made me feel at home. I made a few friends that we still keep in touch with to date and in 3 days I was on my way back to Kenya with a few days stopover in Mogadishu. The stop at Mogadishu was part of work, not leisure. At that point in time I did not think it was an ideal place to go to the beach. But it was an ideal place to make some money.

What I realized working in Somalia is that the value of my services tripled. I was paid close the 3 times what I was paid while working in Kenya. That is what made the risks worth taking.

Back at home things were working out quite well. I even had a girlfriend that I met less than two weeks before I started my Somalia trips. Her name was Dorry; besides many other qualities her height was enough to crown her as a rare beauty. We were still in the stages of getting to know each other when I first travelled to Somalia. A month later we had something serious going on and we had great plans for the future.

My construction project was also falling into place. On 26th July 2016 I was able to fully fund the purchase of the machine required to make the soil building blocks. I was so excited about it for it was my first six digit investment and risk in equal measures. But the latter did not fall under my radar; there was no way this project could fail. The worst case scenario was my parents getting a decent cost friendly house and keep the machine for the next build.

My dad was the man on ground so I organized for a detailed training on how to use the machine and use the technology for building. The plan was to have him trained and therefore train someone else with whom he would work with. He was also excited about it and looking forward to getting it started. My second visit to

Hargeisa came in time just as I had finished getting my dad started with the construction project.

We (a colleague at work and I) were going to do an office networking project and we would be there for more than 2 weeks. Being a big fan of first times I must say this was the first time to spend half a month outside Kenya. Unlike the first visit, I had ample time to explore Hargeisa City and see what it had to offer. Eating and sampling of the local cuisine was a priority; am a foodie and I have no apologies for that.

By the time I was going back home, my dad had not made any progress with the construction project and this was scaring the nuts out of me. I did a few peep talks and a few motivation chats to give him a kick and approach the matter with the same urgency as I did. Hope is all I had and I trusted his capability to make it work. He is quite a go getter and I could not expect less from him.

Meanwhile, the Somalia contracts were escalating and I was needed to go back to another site. This time it would be more than a month in a foreign country as it was a bigger project. It is this project that would change the entire course of my life. First we had a big disagreement with my employer about the compensation and terms of working in Somalia. We did not reach a conclusion that suited me and I resorted to let go of the Somalia jobs and let my other colleagues do it if they were okay with the terms. Unfortunately none had the relevant travel documents and being a team player, I compromised my standards for the team. I decided to undertake the assignment on the condition that I will never be assigned to Somalia again not unless on different terms.

Baidoa was worse than Garowe. I thought I had seen it all when I went to Garowe but little did know the situation could get worse. The airport was in the midst of a highly protected UN camp.

Once you get there on a plane, there was no seeing the outside of those walls unless you are on the plane headed somewhere. In Garowe I had the privilege to stay in a hotel, but not in Baidoa. Baidoa has been a hotbed of conflict from civil war of 1990's to the current fight against the Al-Shabaab led by Ethiopian Military.

The Camp was under the guard of armed private security forces from the inside and the Ethiopian Military from the outside. The Military had a job to keep the militia group as far away from the camp as possible. They were advancing the fight away from the camp and the Baidoa town at large. Being in the camp all seemed to be okay but I realized that all was not well by the scores of the injured soldiers that were seen in the camps health facility.

I do not know if it was a good thing but I was kind of at peace knowing that someone out there was risking their lives to make sure that the UN camp will not come into harm's way. I would definitely not count this as an enjoyable experience but what it accomplished in my life was quite phenomenal and I therefore can never forget. I came here unwillingly but this was a blessing in disguise. I was to meet someone I never knew existed and because of them my life was to change for the better.

I would have loved to share about the work I was doing in Baidoa or any other place for that matter but trust me it is boring. You do not want to hear about it. You do not want to hear the stories of cables and how they were being handled, used or installed. I am also as sure as the sky is blue that you did not pick up this book to learn how computer networks works. With that said and done I will save the both of us some trouble and skip that. Just know it was a tough job working under the 35 degrees sun of Baidoa.

The beauty of being in the camp was the ease of making friends and connecting to several people. The small village syndrome made it easy to know almost anyone whom you meet. There were those people you come across twice or thrice per day. We were all from different backgrounds but we understood each other: we were living in the same situations. Most people were either from Kenya or Uganda. The Ethiopian Military were not as social as we civilians and we respected their space.

To keep me company on a daily basis, I had my phone and its earphones. I was listening to my favorite speaker of all time Les Brown back to back. There was a single tape by him that I played at least 300 times. Up to date, the words of that tape are so clear in my memory till date. The power of hearing and hearing it again and again was tapped into.

The other person I earnestly listened to was the late Dr. Myles Munroe. I had one of his sermons titled The Principles of Success. I cannot quantify the number of times I listened to it but it was enough to tap into the teachings.

Being an Islamic state, the weekends started on Friday to Saturday unlike the usual Saturday and Sunday. Sunday was a working day here. One of the Fridays, bored and frustrated with the living situation, I visited a Kenyan friend to borrow a movie or two to pass time.

What I found instead was a huge playlist with several sermons by the best Gospel teacher of our century, the Late Dr. Myles Munroe. I had always wished to get to learn from him on a deeper level. I had already exhausted the principles of success sermon and these would mean the world to me.

Remember I was a personal development knowledge junkie. Anything that would benefit me by increasing my knowledge or the wisdom I consumed. At this point in time I was hungrier for information that was real life and spiritual. Myles Munroe is all I needed.

A guy who had written over 60 books and 49 of which were bestsellers was just the right person to learn from. The first video I watched was the interview he did while he was in Kenya hosted by the one and only Jeff Koinange. He started oozing wisdom from the word go.

He started by saying that every successful person has a story that does not relate to the success they currently enjoy. He briefly narrated his background where he was brought up. Super humbling, I must admit. I could see myself as he narrated his story, I related with every part of it.

Without knowing I had started owning my own story just like he had owned his. As the story of his life unfolded I realized I had a better upbringing than he did. At least I did not have a teacher call me a monkey or a half breed nigga.

I was wired into his teachings and I dedicated all my free time to learn from him and write notes while at it. I heard scriptures from the Bible that I never knew existed. I heard of a different perspective of seeing things than I ever thought practical. He was a guy teaching, not just with human wisdom but being strongly backed by scripture which I call the God's mind. Up to this point in my life I was learning things that were taught from people's minds but now I had a chance to hear from God's perspective.

It could not have come to me at a better time, remember I just had disagreement with my boss and I had started questioning my need to be employed. I had started asking myself questions like, would I die if I never worked for someone? Would I be sued for refusing to be employed and seek to build my own business? Did I come to this world to just go to work for someone else's dream, get a salary, pay bills and repeat the cycle till I die? What is life all about?

I thank God almighty that I had already gotten disturbed by my life as it was. I know if I was not I could not have listened to Myles Munroe as I did. And if I did not listen to him at that time, I am sure I could not be writing this right now. I believe when you are ready for something (read being sick and tired of being sick and tired of the current circumstances) time, chance and providence make a haste meeting and present all that you need to change. It happened to me and my life took a totally different course.

Myles Munroe through his sermons helped me to understand life from a spiritual view point. First it was a teaching from the book Genesis from the creation story.

I learnt that we were created to dominate the earth; the resources in it and also lead in our own unique ways through tapping into our gifts and talents. Nobody was created as a follower, nobody was created to be a slave, and nobody was created to be dominated by someone else. This made light bulbs to go on in my head. You mean God created us all to be leaders in our own unique ways!

Then I started debriefing my past life. Did I live as a leader or had I allowed the system of the world to dictate what I should do and what I should not do? Was I dominating any resource that I had or was letting someone else dominate it?

I realized I did not dominate my own time as the biggest resource we have as humans. I did not dominate my own talents and gifts, I had rented them to the system of the world for a menial pay. I did not dominate the opportunities and chances I got, I had a boss to answer to and his system did not allow me to pursue anything else. I did not dominate my own life; the quality of life I lived was measured by how much my employer thought I was worth. Someone called the shots in my life unbeknownst to me and I was okay with it! I was shocked at the truths about my life that were being revealed to me at this time.

Of course I had a feeling that I was not living the best life I could live but I was in a system that praised and worshipped my circumstances. A system whereby being an employee was considered the best blessing and being against employment was considered unconstitutional.

I had conformed to the system of the world without my knowledge but here comes a moment of epiphany. I realized that employment was created by human need to dominate other human beings; of which is not the intention of the creator. God created us and deployed us; each person with unique gifts and talents to become a leader not over people but over their area of gifting.

This knowledge gave me sleepless nights, I remembered all the efforts I put into finding my talents earlier in life. I tried writing rap music, I failed, I tried becoming a poet, I did not do well, and I played basketball to mention but a few. But nothing really stood out in me. I was yet to pinpoint my talents and gifts. Meeting Myles Munroe meant that I would make great steps towards finding my gifts.

The learning continued. I learnt that the key to life is finding the area of our gifting which gives you the foundation of your purpose. A person's purpose becomes the source of their personal leadership. In other words, they dominate the earth as per the divine design. Dominating means to lead, manage, master, control, govern and to rule a kingdom. So does God intend us to all have our own kingdoms to dominate? To me the answer was a resounding Yes! He created us to be leaders, simple.

Then I was introduced into the concept of vision and purpose. I remember the first statement he made. "Every manufacturer creates a product to fill an already established purpose" he said. In other words he meant that a manufacturer first encounters a problem that needs a solution and then goes to work to create a product that would perfectly fill that need.

Consequently purpose precedes creation or manufacturing. We can therefore conclude that every good manufacturer will only create a product if it has a purpose; otherwise they would not create it.

On top of that every genuine manufacturer creates a product and then equips it with a manual so that it can guide the operation and handling of the product. The manual states the product's purpose, how it should be handled, how it should be maintained, and all that appertains to effective use of the product. Then it also states the basic principles that govern the product workability that must be strictly followed.

If it is a car, they state it should be fueled with unleaded gasoline or diesel to give an example. Relating this to my life Myles brought it to my attention that God is my manufacturer. Of course I knew that but I never related it to modern day manufacturing industry. Being a wonderful manufacturer, purpose preceded my creation.

That means I was not mass produced by chance but handpicked and custom made for a particular purpose that only I can fulfill. Then being an awesome manufacturer, God brought this way with a manual that would govern our operations. This manual confirms the purpose that brought me this way: earth and gives instructions on what to do, what not to do, where and how to do it and all that is necessary to us as human beings. I call the manual the Bible.

Then I learnt that vision is seeing the purpose manifested. I realized the need for a man to have a dream and a vision. Because purpose is the work that we are required to do but vision gives the work life; it gives the purpose a conceptual reality. But it is important to note that true vision is founded in a divine purpose.

While I was learning all this I became super overwhelmed by the knowledge simply because I did not know my own purpose. All I had was blurry pictures created by wishful thinking. I wanted to be a successful businessman but that did not motivate me as a purpose should motivate us. I wanted to continue learning but I also needed to pinpoint my purpose like yesterday. I was feeling like I had wasted years of my life climbing a ladder lying on the wrong wall. I felt the urgency to plug into my purpose and do something every day towards living that purpose.

Myles Munroe messed me up in good way and I was now in a point of no return. I had confirmed what I always felt inside of me and I realized I was young enough to seek for my divine assignment. I started looking back to when I was in high school and realized I did not have a compelling urge to do anything specific in life.

When I chose to pursue engineering as a career it was not out of a compelling need to serve in the communication industry. Actually for a moment I felt like I did it to prove to myself that I could do well in Mathematics. That did not sound like a purpose, besides the job I was holding did not feel like I was serving a higher cause, higher than myself.

I will dedicate the last chapter of this book to talk about the lessons I learnt from this moment onwards and how I have applied them in my life. I will also share how the future looks like and what my purpose is, which is the main reason I am writing this book.

"One of the greatest tragedies in life is to watch potential die untapped." – Myles Munroe

---

CHAPTER 7

BECOMING

The Baidoa visit was fruitful personally and also for my employer. We did a good job though I returned to Kenya half way. I went back to honor my pact that I would not work in Somalia with the current terms. At least I had given them a reasonable time of 45 days to find someone else. The plan was to go back to Kenya, work on local assignments and be close to my girlfriend Dorry. Little did I know what was waiting for me when I got back home?

When I got back my dad had already made a milestone with the construction project but he had bigger bad news than the good news of getting started. He was complaining that the project was a tough one and he did not think that he had capacity to operate it. This time he was serious about it and knowing my dad he meant every word. I was caught pants down and I had to act quickly to savage my investment. The only solution was to take the bull by its horns.

The solution was to take a step of faith and quit my job with a plan to pursue my Network Marketing Business and my construction business. The decision to quit employment came as a surprise to me, my family and friends in equal measures. I thought I would work for at least 5 years before calling quits and explore my entrepreneurial ambitions. But now here I was, in debt and unprepared but in faith I knew somehow I would figure it out and I would succeed.

Another reason why I was confident enough to quit my job was as a result of the teaching I received from Myles Munroe and months upon months of reading books and consuming all form of personal development material. I was at a moment when I asked myself, if I do not take the risks I want to take in life now that I do not have much responsibilities, how can I do it when I have people dependent on me? (Read family) I also strongly felt that

I was not living a purposeful life and I got a chance to reinvent myself. So I took it knowing that the only life I might be putting at risk was mine. I was confident with only myself to worry about; the uncertainties could be managed easily. I knew it was the right time to start afresh and give myself a shot to become more than I was becoming in employment.

The year 2017 came in fast and furious. This is the year I was to get fully introduced to myself. This is the year I was to find out what I was made of. I was used to a hand to mouth lifestyle where a boss paid me a salary just enough for the basics. Now I was officially outside that safety net and boy, did I know what was waiting for me on this avenue of life? I thought I did but as an old saying goes, you will never know if a bird can fly until you let it out of the cage.

It was time to test my wings and my flight that I believed God instilled in me at birth. It was an avenue I never walked in before and none of my blood relatives had. It was a sail through the unchartered waters of entrepreneurship. I was proud of myself for having the courage to do something that most people will go into the grave without having gathered the guts and I was also scared that I had screwed up my life for good.

I had two voices in my head; one was telling me that I was going to make it and the other was ridiculing me for thinking I had all it takes to become an entrepreneur. The latter must have been the voice of the darkness and the former the voice of the truth and light. I followed the voice of the truth and light. The more I listened to it the weaker the voice of darkness grew.

From experience I knew that if I focused on something and leave no stone unturned I would succeed in it. I was confident that I would replace my salary through my Network Marketing Business in a matter of 3 months or less. I had the skills to make it happen, the network to facilitate it and the attitude to attract it.

What could go wrong?

The plan was to develop a steady income in this business and then send some focus into running the construction business. The latter was not a business I would dedicate my full time efforts on because I had a different idea of what I wanted to become in the long term.

I did not want to spend a moment in my life climbing the ladder leaning on the wrong wall. That was one of the reasons I quit employment, so I just could not get myself into that kind of a trap.

The only reason I kept the construction business idea alive was because I had a debt to pay and I wanted to prove to my dad that it could be done. I had not given up on him yet. I knew he would make a big success out of it sooner or later. In the meantime I was just to keep the dream alive until he could see it.

After three months of hard work on my Network Marketing Business, I did not get the results I thought I would get. I was not earning enough money to pay the most basic of my bills. Armed with the fact that God's delays are not God's denials, I pushed the goal further.

At this point in time I was living on the money owed to me by my former employer. It was close to $2,000 that is Ksh. 200,000 and it was to be paid bit by bit. I was receiving small checks almost every month and that kept a roof over my head and my stove burning so that I did not sleep on an empty stomach. But how long would that money last me in a city where the cost of living is gluttonously high?

From the same money I was paying the loan installments for the now stalled construction business. So it was urgent that I create a source of income and do it fast. In my network marketing company I know I would have been voted as the most likely to succeed because I had all it took for me to make it big in the business. Why do I say this so confidently? Because the people I trust told me so and I also felt it that I was well equipped to make it happen. But the results continued to prove me otherwise.

"The fastest runner doesn't always win the race, and the strongest warrior doesn't always win the battle." Ecclesiastes 9:11 NLT

Six months into my network marketing business I was still struggling to get the traction I needed to propel myself further. I was running behind my bills and life was getting tough on me. Out of desperation I resorted to sell the soil block making machine which was the heart of the construction business.

I needed to sell it and at least settle my loan so that I have one less thing to worry about. I tried networking in efforts of getting a buyer and even put it up on the popular OLX platform hoping to close a deal. Several months later I still had the machine and no one wanted to buy it.

At this moment in time I was officially broke, I could not pay the loan installments and the little money I got was hardly enough to pay my essential bills. In a nice way I had to stop worrying about the loan and focus on living and keeping my eyes on what I wanted to achieve.

In such a situation most people would go running to their former employers like the prodigal son begging to be taken back but that was my last option. I was set on a course that would change the course of my family and impact the world.

The thing that would stop me was not being broke or going to bed hungry. The only thing that would stop me was death. There was no way I was going back in that cage I so much fought to get myself out of.

Around October of 2017, I read a book by Jack Canfield titled *"How to Get from Where You Are to Where You*

Want to Be." This book changed my perspective on the approach I had taken in realizing my full potential.

It reinforced the teachings I got from Dr. Myles Munroe about living with purpose and with intention.

It gave me actionable simple ways to really identify my strengths and therefore pinpoint what I wanted to be, to have and the things I wanted to stand for. From this book I was able to make my mission statement for the first time. This was the conception of *"The Amerucan Dream"* as it is right now.

I realized my strengths were in giving insights, knowledge, wisdom and communication. Then I realized I had a burden to guide, encourage, teach and inspire people.

On top of it I had a burden to push for purposeful living through the God-given gifts that we all possess. *"The Amerucan dream"* was being birthed and I loved the sense of confidence it gave me.

I had my doubts because even after identifying what I really wanted to do with my life, I was not sure if I had what it takes to handle it.

My thinking was, for me to inspire and encourage people I had to have achieved quantifiable amount of success as an entrepreneur. So the plan was to make my network marketing business work, become successful and famous. Then start on my purpose of inspiring people, guiding them to live with purpose and pursue their "Amerucan dreams" or whatever they might baptize their purpose.

But I was struggling to make it in the network marketing industry. My struggle meant that I had to hold onto my purpose longer than I thought necessary. It was painful but it was the only way.

Around the same time, I had invested my time into building a social media following in efforts to expand my reach with my network marketing business products. Instagram became a great escape for me, I was interacting with people who might be interested in my business and I was confident that it would be my breakthrough.

Building an Instagram following organically is not a walk in the park but I have never been afraid of getting my hands dirty for something worthwhile.

All this long, I continued fuelling my purpose, exploring ways and means I could serve it to the world and offer value. I thought of becoming a motivational speaker, but in my understanding, I needed to be successful in life to even think of motivating anyone. So to satisfy this urge in me I utilized the trainings we had at my network marketing company to use my gift.

At those meetings growth was more important than how much success one had achieved. I saw a great platform to grow my speaking skills, presentation skills and once in a while storytelling skills. I remember the joy such opportunities gave me. I always looked forward to being given a chance to speak.

My speaking role model was (and is till to date) Les Brown and I listened to him on daily basis to get his skills by induction. I was becoming a world class speaker but my failure to succeed was putting a stall on my dream to inspire the masses. Instagram was fun but results came in too slowly.

It was my Hail Mary in my network marketing business so I had to do it. The efforts to sell the block making machine were also futile and I was getting deeper into debts. I was in a situation of borrowing to eat; I was at the rock bottom of my life.

Thank God for my warrior attitude, I could have quit chasing my dream and backslid to the safety net of employment.

Family and friends were all worried about what I was doing with my life. Though no one ever mentioned it I think some thought I had become a drug addict or some addiction of some kind that took all my money.

The going got tough with my girlfriend Dorry and I felt the gap in our directions of life. I needed someone to understand and support my efforts to expand myself but to some extent she did not see it.

I could not blame her.

It is human to question someone who has been watering the grounds for a while with nothing coming out of it. It is human to question a tree that is not bearing fruit even when all the seasons have been conducive.

In November 2017, I could hardly pay my rent. Actually I had two months arrears and the situation was getting worse. In all these I kept interacting with my tele-mentors through their books, YouTube videos and audio tapes.

They kept me sane and reminded me that my situation was part of the process of becoming who I wanted to become. They all had a story that I could relate to my current situation. Armed with such knowledge and counting on God, I never lost sleep over my lack. I lived it up like all was well and very few people, if any, really knew the situation I was in.

December 2017, there was no light at the end of the tunnel despite all my efforts. At this point in time, I revisited my construction business idea. I asked myself, what if this was the breakthrough I was hoping for? What if that is where my success would come from? The only way to find out was to try.

A childhood friend had started a successful construction business in my home county, Meru, and I got the idea of pitching my technology to him and then strike a deal of some sort. He is like a brother and I knew there was no way he would turn down a sensible deal.

I decided to shift to my home county from Nairobi city and to pursue the business idea that I so much knew how it was needed there. I did not have the bus fare to make the move so I reached out to my sister who was very supportive in all my struggles. She sent me the money and I made the shift.

Looking back I knew that it was a move of cowardice. I was not moving to the upcountry to only pursue my construction business idea, I was also escaping from the pangs of my purpose. I knew what I wanted to do but I was too naïve and thought I needed to be stinking rich to pursue my purpose. I was also running from the city life because it had gotten really tough on me. This was me quitting and that is why I am saying it was out of cowardice.

I spent the whole of December at home planning and figuring ways and means to get started in the business. We got into heated conversations with my dad who did not like the baggage I had carried about the failed business. He also did not like the fact that I left everything to come pursue something he knew would not work.

But did I listen? I engaged my friend to propose business but instead of marrying my idea all he did was offer me a casual job. Of course I needed a source of income but I was in need of something bigger. Nevertheless I took it but I only stayed long enough to do only one assignment.

At this point in time, I was reading the famous *"Awaken the Giant Within" By Anthony Robbins*. This book was talking about belief systems, life values, rules we set for ourselves, references we for what we believe in and how they affect our identity, emotions, health, social life, finances and general life.

I realized I had some limiting beliefs of what I could become and what I could do. I was a personal development junkie who had no real power to turn the potential power he had in terms of knowledge into a workable plan. Being at home gave me the peace of mind I needed to do the overhaul soul search. I asked myself quality questions and I expected quality answers. Of course they did not come right away.

Here comes the year of our Lord 2018, still in upcountry and no sense of direction in my life. My plans for the construction business were never executed. Number one because I did not know how; my hope was the friend who did not seem to buy the idea. And number two because it was not what I really wanted to do. I did it out of desperation and pain of investing so much money into something and then letting it just sit there.

On January 20th 2018 my network marketing company had a convention for the whole of East Africa in Nairobi. I had already paid for it earlier in the previous year so missing it was not an option. On 17th January, I took a loan from my *Mshwari* Account to cater for the travel expenses to Nairobi and back.

I did not have any other source of income and borrowing from my parents was out of question. I took as much as I could in knowledge that it might take a while to repay it. Besides, I had a bigger debt, this was nothing but peanuts.

On 18th I travelled back to Nairobi. This day my life would be transformed in a big way that I never anticipated. Coming to Nairobi was a matter of attending the convention and then travel back to Meru after a day or two.

The plan was that simple.

I had not given up on building something for myself in Meru. It was on a Thursday and we usually had business trainings in the afternoon at the company's premises. I had missed the sessions so I passed by. Surprising I was called upon to share my story and how social media has impacted my business. I took the opportunity and gave my world class think-on-your-feet short speech.

After the meeting, a colleague introduced me to one of his new team mates; Anna, who as interested to hear more about social media and network marketing business. I did not have enough time to tell her all about it but we exchanged contacts to share more on a later date.

I was in hurry to go meet my girlfriend whom we had reconciled and refocus our energy to making our relationship work. Unfortunately she stood me up on that day but she promised to come to the convention with me. That was all I wanted and I definitely liked the idea.

On the day of the convention she was not picking my calls or replying to my messages. This did not stop me from having fun at the convention. It was a case to sort out later. We learnt a lot, I cannot remember anything in particular, but just so you know it was a great convention.

In the evening after convention I talked to my girlfriend Dorry hoping to get a genuine reason why she did not show up for me when I needed her but all that followed sounded like excuses. We were definitely walking on different paths leading to different directions. More than ever I was convinced that we would never make our relationship work. I was contemplating breaking up with her.

Remember the new friend that I met two days earlier and wanted to learn more about social media? Yeah, her name is Anna. We did not talk until the evening after the convention. We started by getting to know each other before we could dive right into the social media thing.

Somewhere along the way, the getting to know each other revealed several things we had in common and it got exciting. We forgot the business part and stuck with getting acquainted. We concluded that we needed to meet over a cup of coffee to continue with the conversation and probably talk about social media.

Meeting Anna was a big blessing as well as an eye-opener. For me she was just a lady who wanted my social media expertise. But I found out she was an angel sent by God to bring life back to my life.

I cannot say what she did, or what she said to me, but I knew with absolute certainty that she impacted my life in a great positive way. That is what angels do, right? We cannot explain it but we feel their impact.

After meeting Anna, it was clearer to me what I wanted out of life and I was out to pursue it. First was to end a relationship that I felt was going nowhere. Second it was to re-evaluate my decision to move to upcountry and face life as it was in the city because this was where my future lay.

So I tried to setup a date to break up with Dorry in an understandable and decent way but she would not show up. I tried calling, she would not pick. I was in a hurry to shift the direction of my life before hopelessness overtook me so I did it over a text message.

I know it is not a decent way to break up with someone but what could I have done? Kidnap her for a date? Besides I really wanted to see her hoping she would give me a reason why we could make it work because I did not have any. I was not ready to let her go yet. But she forced my hand.

I then made a call back home and let my folks know that I had decided to stay a little longer than I anticipated. I met Anna almost on a daily basis, yes I liked her that much but also she inspired me in a way I cannot explain.

Being around her was more than therapeutic. She asked about my dreams and my plans in life. She was interested to hearing about the mistakes I had done in life and she listened to understand not to judge. She saw something in me and asked questions like, why have you not done this already?

She got me uncomfortable in a way I admired and longed for. She put up some fire under my seat and forced me to stand up.

A week after meeting Anna, I reached out to another friend I had met on Instagram a while back. She was my potential client and she also became a friend. On that Saturday morning she told me that she was going for a talk that was happening in Nairobi CBD and she called it Centonomy Open Day.

I never miss such events if I qualify to attend. I asked her what the requirements were and I found out it was free. As fast as my body could move I prepared myself to attend an event that had already started. That is how much I value information.

By the time I got at the venue it was already 11am and the final speakers were being called to stage. The hall was fully packed and you could feel the importance and the weight of matters being talked about.

I had learnt that Centonomy offers education on personal finance management and wealth creation. When I sat down the MC took to the podium and called Mr. Douglas Waudo, who was a founder of an organization that I did not quite get the name, and a communication specialist. He was an alumnus of the Centonomy Program.

Listening to Mr. Douglas Waudo speak I realized what I had always wanted in a mentor. He was not famous but he had things going on for him. He was not from a well up family but against all odds he was living a life that most people would only wish for.

He spoke with confidence because of his faith in God and his experience in life. I really wished that we would get to know each other in person. I saw my future through him and I prayed that our paths may cross in one way or another. I knew trying to meet him after the session would have been superficial or worse unproductive. So I just let the matter rest with God.

I was greatly blessed by his story; how he overcame poverty, bad habits and what he was doing with his life.

Next on stage was the founder of Centonomy, Madam Waceke Nduati.

She narrated how she started her company from a very humble beginning. What stood out most for me is when she confessed that when she started coaching people on how to manage their finances, she was in debt and had no logical experience to be telling people how to handle their finances. All she had was information and an attitude to make it irrespective of the facts.

To me this was a slap in the face. There I was thinking that I needed to be successful in order to inspire other people to do the same. That was such a backward kind of thinking and I was suffering because of it.

Thanks to Anna for keeping me around longer and my Instagram friend for inviting me to the event. There I made the decision that I will not tie my purpose with the degree of the success I have achieved or not achieved in life.

I made it clear that no matter what happens with my other businesses, I will pursue my purpose; *"The Amerucan Dream."*

Afterwards on our way out we were handed some brochures that I only kept because of their excellent quality. I did not read it right away but I knew I would, sooner than later. It was about a mentorship program named Living Effectively Mentorship Program (LEMP).

I learnt that it was founded to provide mentorship opportunities to people committed to personal and professional development. I related with everything it stood for and I made a quick decision to attend one of its sessions to see what it was about.

LEMP came to my life at the right time to stamp what I always knew but was afraid of living up to. I realized their main goal was to equip individuals to discover their purpose and maximize their God-given potential to live effectively on earth as they also become agents of change.

This is exactly what I needed to propel my life to the next level. My construction business had failed and left me in debts, my network marketing business did not seem to grow. It was time to move on and do that thing that I would die for; my purpose.

I had already pinpointed my purpose but what LEMP did was to relate it with God's plan. Through the scriptures I was still able to discover the same purpose as I had earlier identified. This was a great assurance of why I was born. I not only believed it, but I also had evidence from the creator. I had certainty that impacting people through talking to them was my purpose and this fact strengthened *"The Amerucan Dream."*

On top of that I found out that the guy I admired at the Centonomy open Day, Mr. Douglas Waudo, was the founder of the mentorship program. My prayer to get to meet him and get acquainted was answered. He became a great friend and a brother to me.

After completing the mentorship program I met him to share my vision so that he would guide me. He was so thrilled to hear how closely related our purposes were. He then challenged me to start up an organization of my own no matter how humble. This would see the birth of the vehicle that would carry *"The Amerucan Dream."*

2018 was a transformative year for me. It reminds me of how a caterpillar transforms into a butterfly. I had the same kind of Metamorphosis, I saw myself step out of my comfort zone and resolved to stay put for better or for worse until I can fully manifest my purpose. With the support from my new friend and mentor Douglas and my newly found angel Anna, I knew I would make it.

It was also a tough year but thank God I had a sense of mission, nothing deterred me. I was well fed spiritually by LEMP and I personally made efforts to know God better. My network marketing business was providing enough for basic needs but nothing more. I learnt to be content with little and without. In everything I thanked God and I knew greater things were in my future.

"As iron sharpens iron, so a friend sharpens a friend." Proverbs 27:17 [NLT]

Talking of my future, the path I wanted to take was clear. *"The Amerucan dream"* was defined and refined. It was ready to be executed after the necessary planning. Being Frank the organization that I registered to carry the dream was set to go.

The mission of Being Frank was *"The Amerucan Dream"* itself; *Educating towards Abundance and Prosperity.*

A mission that came about after I took an X-ray scan of my entire life and found out that I grew up in a scarcity mindset.

I grew up knowing there was not enough money. I grew up knowing there were not enough opportunities. I grew up knowing there were not enough resources. I grew up knowing there were not enough talents for everyone since I struggled to find my own.

I grew up knowing of only one way to make it in life; going to school, getting good grades and consequently a good, well-paying job. I grew up thinking there were not enough kind and good people in the world.

I grew up thinking that love was a rare thing. I grew up afraid of bad health. A very deep scarcity attitude reigned in me. I knew I struggled in life because of it and that is why I made it my mission to stand up for the very opposite: Abundance.

Moreover in the world we are living in, scarcity is being accentuated.

We are seeing financially successful men and women who have no healthy social life; their marriages fail and there friendships are superficial, religious people who are sick and broke all the time, influential people in the society who have one or two chronic diseases. Etc.

These and many other combinations are leaving us consciously or subconsciously thinking that we cannot have it all in life. But *"The Amerucan Dream"* has a mission to change that attitude and empower people to have it all; a 360 degree abundant life. Good Health,

Spiritually grounded, financial freedom, great relationships and all that appertains to these four major quadrants of life.

"The Amerucan Dream" is here to empower people to define what living a rich life means to them and not what the system of the world has fed them. To define what it means to live a fulfilling life without being slaves to the system of the world. And become all that they were created to be; leaders and the heirs of the kingdom of God.

To do that Being Frank in regards to *"The Amerucan Dream"* will be trying to answer seven questions and then applying the answers to each and every quadrant of life. These questions are:

- *Who Am I?*
- *Where Did I Come From?*
- *Why Am I Here?*
- *What Can I Do?*
- *Where Am I Going?*
- *How Will I Get There?*
- *How Will I Know When I Get There?*

These questions are seven because seven is a number of completeness as well as a spiritual number. It is not by chance, it is the way it should be for us to figure out our course in life. From the first to the last we are trying to find out our Identity, Origin, Purpose, Potential, Destiny,

Planning and Goal Setting Respectively. If I manage to help a soul find those answers, *"The Amerucan Dream"* shall be accomplished.

EPILOGUE

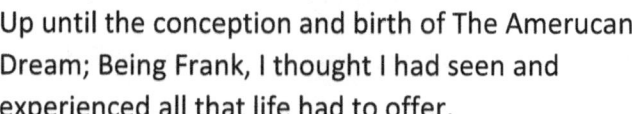

Up until the conception and birth of The Amerucan Dream; Being Frank, I thought I had seen and experienced all that life had to offer.

I thought I had earned myself a Master's Degree in Life through experience. It was a nice thing, feeling such certainty of having life changing experiences at a very young age. I have had the worst of heart breaks.

I have had the worst of grades in school. I have had the worst of humiliation and attacks on whom I was. I had made the worst of financial decisions that left me broke and with no means to provide myself with the basics.

I had travelled to a war zone, worked there and made it back home in one piece. I had interacted with people from different cultures and I befriended some. I had rose from nothing to something in several aspects of my life.

I had overcome my fears and dared to dream big. I had taken the risks that most people my age will never take. I had tried to date the un-datable and befriend the un-friendable.

I had managed to alter the influence of my mother tongue on my speech. I had read more books than most people will ever read in their lifetime. I had listened to inspiration talks and speeches for hours more than most people will spend reading their Bible. I was confident that I had experienced all that life could throw at me.

Could things get any worse, more than they already were?

It was on 3rd March 2018 when I got someone to buy the machine that took me into a financial crisis pit-hole. At that time my priority was to get out of debt, so all the proceeds went to service my loan arrears.

Earlier in the year when I joined a Bible Study Group courtesy of LEMP and my mentor Douglas, my prayer request was financial breakthrough.

Almost immediately the prayers started getting answered and this was one of the answers. I was getting out of debt and my financial life was being rejuvenated. Thank you to God and to the members of LEMP Fellowship for their prayers and support.

To God be the glory for this answered prayer. It was by grace and mercy of the Lord; not by my own efforts.

When the machine was sold, my dad was happier than I was. I realized it bothered him as much as it bothered me. Besides it was our failed construction business. He felt the responsibility for its failure just like I did.

I was happy to get the baggage off both our backs and it was a fresh start for both of us. After this I was unstoppable and I vowed to make my Dad proud with another business venture; the pursuit of *"The Amerucan Dream."*

Then the unthinkable happened.

It was on 19th March 2019 at around 10am. I had woken up early to write the book you have in your hands right now. I cannot quite remember where I was in the writing but it is definitely in the last quarter of the book. I received a call from my uncle from the upcountry; Meru, sounding rather distressed.

Before then, it had been long since we last talked on phone. Out of unknown reasons the call was cut for at least 3 times before he finally broke the news to me. My young, vibrant and ambitious Dad was found dead at work in a neighboring school where he served as a security officer.

I cannot describe the emotion I felt at that time but the best part of me thought it was a sick joke. I even gathered the courage to type a few more lines of this book. But just before I could complete a paragraph, I received another call from another uncle. The reality started to sink immediately; how could they call at almost the same time?

Your guess is as good as mine; I did not pick it up. As if that was not enough a close neighbor from the village called. At this point it was clear; I had lost my dad to unknown reasons. He was ill a while back but he never had a life threatening condition. He was a healthy man all his life. What could have happened? Could it be foul play? But he never had a grudge with anyone; a peace maker he was.

I had a million thoughts running in my head in just a few seconds after which the facts were clear; I had lost my dad and I felt the gap.

Before I could collect the energy to cry, I prayed; God my dad is gone, I do not want to ask why but give me the grace to accept this and move on. Amen.

I cried as hard as I could and regretted all the time I had postponed travelling upcountry to see my parents. I realized how short life was, just a few days earlier I was talking to my dad and we had a plan to meet for some serious men talk. Now I will never know what he had in mind to say to me.

I realized the importance of treating each day as a gift and living it up.

Yes things could get worse and they just did.

I held the bad news as long as I could to first absorb them and counsel myself that it shall all be well and that God had bigger plans for us as a family. I reflected a lot on Jeremiah 29:10 *"For I know the plans I have for you, declares the Lord. Plans to prosper you and not to harm you, plans to give you hope and a future."* [NIV]

This scripture became my comfort and my stand. By the time I was ready to share the news with the friends later in the afternoon, I was quite at peace though really hurting. I realized the importance of the personal development that I had pursued in the last few years. In a greater way I realized the importance of counting on God and casting my cares to him.

The next day I travelled to my village in Meru County where I would remain for two weeks to plan for my dad's funeral.

In the next few days I would learn many things I never knew about my dad or at least I was too blind to see. To me he was the greatest and the best dad in the world. I knew he did other things in the society but I never experienced the magnitude of his societal contributions before now. I thought apart from our family no one else would miss him as much. I was wrong.

In just a few days I heard tributes from people I never knew before of how dad had impacted their lives and those of others around them. They were people from all walks of life, from the villagers and village leaders, to farmer societies, to church, to schools and even friends and distant relatives.

They all narrated how a visionary leader my dad was even in occasions where he was in the follower capacity. Some called him a peace maker who liked to see everything work in harmony and others called him a mentor. Some praised his efforts to advance different organizations and how hard it will be to fill the gap he left.

I had lost my dad but the society had also lost a great leader important to its advancement. This knowledge made the mourning easier because deep down I knew my dad had run a good race and had kept the faith to the end. He had served the world and he had taken care of his family to the best of his ability.

One of the things I was worrying about was the finances to cater for the funeral expenses. But from friends alone we were able to raise more than three times of the funeral budget. I realized how important it was to create great relationships with people and to show up for them when they needed you.

I realized how small gestures towards a friend at the right moment could mean the world to them.

I realized how much he cared for those that showed even a little concern for him.

I realized unknowingly I had picked up the habit of making friends and keeping them from my dad. My own friends came through for me just as much my dad's friends came through for him.

> "Use your worldly resources to benefit others and make friends. Then, when your earthly possessions are gone, they will welcome you to an eternal home." LUKE 16:9 [NLT]

I realized that I had also picked up my loyalty and work ethics from my dad. When the Head Mistress of Nkuene Girls stood to talk and give her tributes I got a revelation. She mentioned how much my dad loved his job in the school as a security officer and how he was true to his assignment with no toleration of mediocrity and all its cousins.

She said that the students loved him and saw him as their father who kept them safe because he positioned himself as such. She said that even the managerial staff sought his advice on matters concerning the operation of the school.

This was deep stuff especially when I thought that my dad was in the job just for the money like many employed people. For him it was a chance to live a purposeful life, to put serve a cause larger than self and contribute his prowess in leadership and management for the good of the society.

Now I realized why he could not handle the construction business that we had started. It would have compromised his ability to do what he loved best and I was too blind to see that. He really loved his job to let anything, even money to get into its way. He loved the students of Nkuene and they were like his children just like we are. He could not imagine leaving them before the law said so; retirement.

What a closure after I struggled too hard to understand why he would bail out on me! Not that I had hard feelings about it but it was such a humbling moment to come to realize that it was his ethics and loyalty that did not allow him to pursue the business idea.

I started to see more clearly how similar I was to dad. No wonder he never used to bother me a lot with lectures why I should look for a job after things went south for me. He knew I was his son and I was like him; I would do what I set out to do or die trying. He understood my stubbornness in implementing my ideas and pursuing what I deemed as my purpose.

Hearing people talk about my dad refreshed the respect I had for him and multiplied it a couple of times. I had always wanted to make him proud just like he worked hard to make us proud. For him he had won the race of making his family proud. We did not cry because he left us in any trouble but we cried because he was not there to hear all the great things said about him. And of course we missed and will forever miss him.

Now that he is no longer here to see what becomes of his firstborn son, mine is to be the best son I can be to my mother, the best brother I can be to my siblings, the best dad I can be to my children and the best husband I can be to my wife (at the writing of this I am single Ha-ha!)

Above all is to carry on his servant leadership legacy and his advance-humanity attitude and take it further from where he was able to reach.

I now have a new role, I can never fit into my dad's shoes but I am the man of the house sitting in his seat. I do not know what it takes to be counted on to make some family decisions but I respect his upbringing and I believe I am empowered.

I do not know what the future holds but I am a dreamer and a visionary; I can see tomorrow and I am sure it shall be well.

I miss my dad, I truly do. I never imagined fathering my children without his guidance. I never imagined becoming someone's husband without his counsel. I never imagined becoming a CEO of my own empire without his fatherly advice. But I will trust in the Lord that he already taught me what I needed to learn from him and what I did not learn, God will reveal it to me in His myriad mysterious ways.

On top of that I will use the sorrow of losing him as the gasoline to fuel *"The Amerucan Dream"* and make it a reality. He passed on knowing that I was onto something that I promised him would change and elevate my life to a different level just like he always wanted for me. I have no choice but to keep my promise to my dad.

> *"I will not violate my covenant or alter the word that went froth from my lips."*
> *Psalms 89:34 [ESV]*

ACKNOWLEDGEMENTS

Putting this book together was not a solo effort. Yes I might have owned the story and knew everything I needed to write but it was not without a support system that I counted on for inspiration, guidance and prayers.

When I conceived the idea to write a book about my journey and name it *"The Amerucan Dream"*, Diana Moseti was the first person I shared it with. Being the great friend she is, she challenged me to go for it and make it a reality. She made frequent follow-ups and kept asking of my progress.

Frankly speaking this was a project I wanted to do the entire of 2019; the goal was to write the last word before 31st of December 2019.But with such a friend who is always nudging you forward, what do you expect? With her on my case and a few other life issues I was able to narrow down it to a mid-year project. I could not have gotten this far, this quick without your loving care and support. Thank you my friend. You will always have a special place in my heart.

To my loving Mum, Grace, you are the best mum in the world. How could you believe in your son so much without any evidence of what he said he was working on? Only you and God can understand that but I am super grateful for being my number one fan. You have always believed in my ideas and you never judged me in my failures. You are heaven sent and I am always grateful to God for you, Mama. Live Long!

To my dad dancing with angels, there is a lot I can say about you but you cannot read it. I will forever be grateful for the man you were, who inspired the man I am and are still becoming. Rest in Peace.

To my siblings: you are the best in the whole world. My sis Carol you have had my back in all the dark stages of my story, I can never repay you my dear. My brother Morris, you have been an inspiration. Continue in your thirst to live a purposeful life and you will never regret it. And my baby sister Millicent; how do you manage to be so mature at your age? You have inspired me to become a better version of myself so that I can be a better brother to you. Thank you for believing in 'Being Frank' and being my fan. I am blessed to have you.

I love you all.

A while even before I was convinced that my life was long enough to fit in a page, a friend had suggested that I write a book. Eliaph Ngari, I do not know if you remember it but you once floated to me the idea to write a book. I know this is a seedling of the seed you planted in me casually a while ago. I will forever be grateful for your friendship and the support I have received from you ever since we met close to a decade ago. Cheers to many more my brother and awesome friend.

My right hand man, my fellow dreamer, I told you I will write a book and instead of laughing at me you gave me an insight of how big it would get. Kenneth Munene, you are a real brother. You gave me hope when my hope faded away; you gave me courage when I was frail. I could not have done this without you brother. We have come from far and further we are going. Thank you!

Jacinta Mwaura, you have been a true friend and a sister in many ways. You have always believed in me and my dreams. You have always supported me in many ways especially when I needed you most. I treasure every second of knowing you. You have immensely contributed to this dream and may the Lord bless you beyond human imagination.

To my brother, friend and mentor Douglas Waudo; where could I be without you? Before I met you I never experienced the reality of my dreams and purpose. Meeting you was the rubber stamp I needed to get the permission to start playing full out. You were indeed heaven sent and I will forever be grateful to God for the gift of you. I am still a work in progress but with you close to me I will get better and better. Thank you for founding Living Effectively Mentorship Program (LEMP).

It has impacted my life and it will impact millions more for the glory of God.

To all the members of LEMP Fellowship group; you know that this book was one of our prayer items. Here it is! Your prayers have been answered and all glory to God for this. He has done it once again. Let us continue to pray and fellowship together as we grow in the presence of the Lord.

To my great friend Raymond Munene. We met at a very crucial stage in my life; I was still seeking to find my footing of whom I was. You were a great desk-mate in high school and a great friend afterwards. Thank you for putting up with my 'villageness' back then and for being someone I can count on up to date.

To Mary Mengo and the entire NeoLife Family, you have been a blessing to my journey. Thank you for believing in me and holding my hand when I needed it most. God bless you all.

Lastly, to all the people; friends, associates, clients, colleagues and family who came into my life and made me a better person; I appreciate you. You have been a special part of my journey and I could not have had it otherwise. Be it the drama or the life changing conversations, I appreciate.

More importantly I acknowledge my tele-mentors Robert T. Kiyosaki, Napoleon Hill, Stephen Covey,

Anthony Robbins, Les Brown, Lisa Nichols, Grant Cardone, Eric Worre, Jack Canfield, Brendon Burchard, Dale Carnegie, Gary Vaynerchuk, Myles Munroe, Joel Osteen and all the authors and speakers of the awesome books I have read and the awesome speeches I have listened to respectively. I could not be where I am without your genius insights in different topics.

Thank you all for all your unique efforts in the making of this book.

APPENDICES

Miraa - Khat

Toka nitoke – Twins

Githeri - a mixture of boiled maize and beans

Ugali - Cornmeal mush

Mukima Tree - Gravillea

Zilizopendwa - Old school tunes

Sukumawiki – Collard greens

Penye miti hapana wajenzi - Where there are plenty of trees there are no builders

Soko - Market

Muratina drink/kithiri - Local brew

Muratina tree - Sausage tree

MauMau - Freedom fighters

Kimeru - Native language of the Meru people, Kenya

Panga - A long knife with a broad blade used as a cutting tool in Africa

Asiyesikia la mkuu huvunjika guu - Swahili proverb meaning he who does not heed the warnings of his superiors ends up regretting

MIA – Missing in action

Pishori rice - fine quality long grain rice cultivated in the rich soils of Mwea, Kenya

Semo – Seminary

Vitu Vizuri – Good things

Acha niende nikarare/ Naenda kulala – refers to bedtime
Diss – Criticize/ Dismiss

Shamba – Garden

Nairobians – Native dwellers of Nairobi city

Eldy – Abbreviation for Eldoret town

Chips mwitu – Cheap Street French fries

Chapatis - an unleavened Kenyan flatbread filled with flaky soft layers and pan-fried until golden

Wendo – Love

Dada - Sister

Mshwari – a banking product for M-PESA customers for borrowing money through their phone

Let's connect on Social media?

QUICK TIP: Use your Smartphones Google Lens or any other Barcode and QR scanner app.

Instagram

- Click https://bit.ly/BeingFrankOnIG or

- Scan

Facebook

- Click https://bit.ly/BeingFrankOnFB or

- Scan

YouTube

- Click https://bit.ly/BeingFrankOnYouTube or

- Scan

Twitter

- Click   https://bit.ly/BeingFrankOnTwitter or

- Scan

Website

- Click Click <https://beingfrank.co.ke/> or

- Scan

www.ingramcontent.com/pod-product-compliance
Lightning Source LLC
LaVergne TN
LVHW041249080426
835510LV00009B/660